DIGITAL PERSUASION

DIGITAL PERSUASION

SELL SMARTER IN THE MODERN MARKETPLACE

ERIN GARGAN

LIONCREST
PUBLISHING

DIGITAL PERSUASION
Sell Smarter in the Modern Marketplace

ISBN   978-1-61961-825-1 *Paperback*
       978-1-61961-826-8 *Ebook*

Dedicated to the memory of Raymond Wtulich.
Ray was a valued client and friend, and the marketing
visionary who inspired me to write this book.

CONTENTS

INTRODUCTION

How long do you have to capture someone's attention?

Exactly the time it takes them to read this sentence.

Ten words. Two and a half seconds of reading.

In the digital age, this is the length of time you have before someone decides if you are worth their time. It's how long you have before they decide whether you are worth listening to, worth considering, or worth a response.

Ten words is the average length of a mobile notification. Ten words is the average combination of subject line and message preview, or sender name and message preview.

Ten words is how long someone will take to subconsciously decide whether or not to open your email, post, message, or text. You have *one* sentence, in this digital age, to attract someone's attention and stand out from an overcrowded inbox. One sentence stands between being ignored and igniting a new opportunity.

What can you *possibly* type in ten words to persuade someone to give you a chance?

Luckily, the answer lies waiting for you right here in this book. Welcome to the art of digital persuasion.

You've probably heard the statistic that most people have the attention span of a goldfish.

One of my favorite authors, Sally Hogshead, shares that we have nine seconds in the real world to "fascinate" someone. You're probably thinking this idea is panic-inducing enough, but let's consider how those real-world interaction windows translate inside the digital environment.

How have we gone from great communicators to goldfish? Hysteria rises every year, with each new research study shaving a second off our attention spans from the year before. Entrepreneurs, sales professionals, and marketers scramble for solutions to attract and hold digital eye contact with their most targeted prospective customers. Phone books and landlines, communication pillars of the last century, have all become extinct. But why?

The answer? A chocolate-bar-sized device that's probably within your reach right at this very moment.

Ten years ago, Steve Jobs introduced the iPhone to the world—and promptly changed it forever.

Do you remember the days before mobile communication took over our lives and tethered us to this glowing, beeping device? Do you remember when you actually had a real live clock, calculator, flashlight, mirror, camera, and calendar? Just over a decade ago, you may have woken up, read the paper, watched TV, had breakfast, jumped in the car, and headed to the office. Settling in, you may have hit your blinking voicemail button to check any messages from early-bird overachievers. Next up on the day's to-do list? *Check email*—that designated hour or so was "email-checking time." That came after the five minutes it took your desktop computer (complete with CD-ROM tower) to start up, followed by waiting for your email inbox to (slowly) reveal itself to you. With a few sips of coffee, you would dig in. The day's first messaging experience happened around 9 a.m., fifteen hours or so from the last time you enjoyed this fun, newish medium. Then, an hour or so after you'd started, you were probably done. You moved on to whatever was next on your to-do list.

Email was *manageable*—you could read through every message from the day before with careful consideration and reply accordingly. Checking your email was a task you *completed*. It had a start, and it had a finish. Digital messaging didn't follow you through every hour of your day. It wasn't an omnipresent being without beginning or end. It wasn't dinging, whooshing, pinging, playing, and stalking you with alerts every moment of your existence. It was very efficient and effective for business communication.

Let's fast-forward to today. What time did you first check your messages? Was it in the middle of the night when you couldn't sleep? Was it within five minutes of waking up, like sixty percent of today's Americans?[1] Do you keep checking those notifications throughout your morning—while brushing your teeth, making your coffee, getting dressed? By the time you leave for work—or sit down in front of your laptop, if you work from home—have you prepared your brain for another day on the digital communication battlefield?

Digital messaging has become a part of us, with our phones as physical extensions of our hands. If our phones

1   Deloitte, *Global Mobile Consumer Survey: US Edition*, 2017.

aren't in our hands, they're in our pockets, on our tables, or in our bags. Whatever beep, chirp, or ding you have set up as your notification sound is probably branded in your mind and inspires an immediate Pavlovian response: your eyes dive to that little screen and stay glued for as long as it takes to scroll through everything.

We check messages while walking, which is fairly dangerous. We check messages while driving, which is deadly dangerous. Forty percent of us admit to checking messages while using the bathroom, which, while not technically dangerous, is disgusting.[2] We spend five hours a day checking messages on our phones[3] and another two-plus hours on laptops and tablets.[4]

The introduction of the iPhone transformed digital communication from something we leave at the office to something that follows us everywhere. From email to Facebook and from LinkedIn to texting, we are engaging. YouTube, Quora, and Instagram rob us of precious hours

2 John Rampton, "How Many People Use Their Phone in the Bathroom," Inc.com, accessed September 6, 2017, https://www.inc.com/john-rampton/how-many-people-use-their-phone-in-the-bathroom.html.

3 Sara Parez, "U.S. Consumers Now Spend 5 Hours per Day on Mobile Devices," TechCrunch.com, posted March 3, 2017, https://techcrunch.com/2017/03/03/u-s-consumers-now-spend-5-hours-per-day-on-mobile-devices/.

4 Zach Espein, "Horrifying Chart Reveals How Much Time We Spend Staring as Screens Each Day," posted May 29, 2014, http://bgr.com/2014/05/29/smartphone-computer-usage-study-chart/.

we can never get back. The latest attention-grabber is social media "Stories," courtesy of Snapchat and its imitators. Stories demand only seconds of our attention at a time to share moments of our lives.

Is it any wonder we can't stay focused for long when there's so much *demanding* our attention? Every. Single. Moment? Forget attention spans. In the digital age, it's more like we have attention "specks."

Come to think of it, why am I even writing a book in a world like this, where I probably lost you paragraphs ago?

I'm on a mission to improve how persuasive you are every single time you type, text, or tweet. I'm on a mission to eradicate digital sales junk from the face of the digital earth. I want to save you time and rejection. I want to ignite real, profitable business relationships. I want you to persuade the people behind the screen to believe that you should be heard. My goal is to have the inboxes of both senders and receivers of digital messaging full of mutually powerful opportunity-openers—not worthless, irrelevant junk.

So, let's get personal for a moment. Do me a favor: take out your phone. Look at your mail app and social media icons.

Be honest. How many unread messages do you have?

In the world of modern communication, there are three different types of people: Readers, Swipers, and Scrollers.

Readers actually take the time to read, or at least open, each message that hits their inbox, no matter how irrelevant it may be. Swipers immediately swipe to make the message disappear—to the archive, to the trash, or to the "read" status. And Scrollers just roll straight through their inbox, opening only messages they know are relevant or that catch their attention.

Which one are you?

Personally, I'm a Scroller. My friends look at the sky-high number on my mail app's unread badge and think I'm insane. They gasp and act like it's more scandalous than a low credit score or not giving to charity. They assume I must be one of those re-gifters and that I probably don't floss. Am I a bad person for having a high unread-message count? Maybe. Here's what greets me every time I look at the home screen on my phone:

In my defense, the *reason* for having hundreds of thousands of unopened messages is that, in my attempt to tread inbox water without drowning on a daily basis, I've learned that *most messages really suck*. Not yours or mine, of course, but many other messages.

If you're a Scroller like me, you get it.

Most people have their own version of what I call the "inbox wasteland"—that place where unread messages go to languish in obscurity. Mine is a garbage dump full of toxic waste. Swipers' inbox counts might look better at first glance, but, in reality, all they're doing is shoving their unreads in a closet like they're cleaning their house for a surprise visit from the in-laws.

Readers? Well, they're just better people—those whom I aspire to one day be like. They also probably pay their taxes on January 2. Okay, that wasn't fair. If you are a Reader, I'm just jealous of your capacity for perfection.

No matter whether you're a Reader, Swiper, or Scroller, we all have to deal with the inbox wasteland. We all have our personal way of dealing with the onslaught of digital messages that wash over us like waves all day. We're trying to roll with the tide and keep our heads above water.

Most of us just want to cut through the noise enough to find what's important. Many of us outright *ignore* the rest.

MASTERING THE ATTENTION SPECK

If you're someone who has to reach out to people you don't know on a daily basis and persuade them to give you a chance, how do you make yourself heard?

How do we, as entrepreneurs and business development professionals, deal with this attention speck challenge? How can we make the things we type stronger than our recipients' survival instinct geared to tread inbox water with snap judgments? The reality is that most people, even when they want to, don't have the time to be polite and hear every single person out. How can we keep our "Interested in giving me a chance?" messages out of the inbox wasteland?

The first step is understanding message-checking psychology. Think of how you check your email, social, or mobile inboxes. When you and I check our messages, most often we're in efficiency mode. We're leaning in, looking to get to the next message quicker than the last, knocking out emails and notifications, and moving on to another task on our list. How long do your eyes typically stay on a message preview or notification? Just a couple of seconds, right? Your recipients—your potential customers, clients, or partners—are exactly the same.

We're all in the mentality, with each new message, of trying to answer one question as fast as we can: *What do you want?*

In two and a half seconds, fair or not, our brains look at that sender's name and the message preview and, faster than a reality show judge, categorize the sender as one of four people:

1. **Friend:** I know you or think I know you, or you might be a friend of a friend.

   This message gets opened and read almost one hundred percent of the time. This message triggers feelings of "I like, know, and/or trust you; let's continue communicating!"

2. **Foe:** I don't know you and I don't want to know you. You are definitely trying to sell me something I definitely don't need.

   The brain has decided this is social sales spam. This message is typically never opened, let alone read, and gets swiped or scrolled almost one hundred percent of the time. It triggers feelings of digital murder. It's like a video game: *Foe alert! Swipe. Trash.* Nothing is more fun than deleting the bad guys. Cue hero music... One message closer to a peaceful inbox.

3. **Seller:** I don't know you and I'm pretty sure you're trying to sell me something, but there's a small chance it might be something that I want or need.

   Depending on how busy that person's day is, or their frame of mind at that exact moment, this message may or may not get opened. It's a crapshoot. This message triggers feelings of vague annoyance or vague curiosity.

4. **Server:** I don't know you, but you seem interesting and might be someone that could help me. You offered something in a few words that my brain perceived as creative, personal, or useful.

   This message gets opened, and it's typically read in full one hundred percent of the time. This message triggers feelings of reciprocity: "Thank you for helping me. How else could you maybe help me? How can I maybe help you?"

Persuading your recipient's brain within the first ten words of your message, successfully indicating you are either a Friend or a Server, is the art of digital persuasion.

Chances are, you've thought to yourself, *I know I'm being annoying, but I have to be!* Or, maybe you've just never really considered it from your recipient's perspective and, now that you have, you'd rather not be "that person."

Either way, this book will help those feelings be gone forever. You don't have to be annoying. You don't have to be rejected. You don't have to be frustrated. You don't have to do the same thing over and over and get weaker results.

According to several studies, the average number of total emails, texts, social media messages, and other digital messaging that approaches our brains for decision-making on a daily basis is somewhere in the neighborhood of three hundred per day.[5] *Three hundred.* If you're an entrepreneur, executive, or general hustler, you're probably closer to five-hundred-plus.

What most people don't realize is that—because sixty-six percent of all email is read on mobile devices, versus

---

5   Craig Smith, "By the Numbers: 80+ Incredible Email Statistics and Facts," DMR, updated February 14, 2017, https://expandedramblings.com/index.php/email-statistics/; "18-24-Year Old Smartphone Owners Send and Receive almost 4K Texts per Month," Marketing Charts, posted March 21, 2013, http://www.marketingcharts.com/industries/telecom-industries-27993.

thirty-four percent on desktop—all your recipients will likely see of your message is the notification, or maybe the inbox preview.[6] Combined, those usually consist of about ten words, which take about two and a half seconds to read. After two and a half seconds, your brain decides Friend, Foe, Seller, or Server—and based on that near-instantaneous conclusion, your recipient reads, swipes, or scrolls on by.

The fate of your carefully-crafted message, and whether you are categorized as Friend or Server, lies in the hands of just ten typed words. As a frame of reference, that last sentence is more than twice as long as the length of text that will trigger the categorization you want.

Most digital messages are composed and sent with the intention of receiving a yes or no. Here's the catch—there's a step before that action: simply being seen. It's the *step before the step*. It's persuading someone that you are a Friend or a Server. It's persuading someone to take a positive action of any kind. It's persuading someone to stop their scroll.

How to do exactly that is what you'll learn in this book.

---

6   Greg Sterling, "Mobile Devices Drive 66 Percent of Email Opens—Report," Marketing Land, posted May 9, 2014, http://marketingland.com/34-percent-email-opens-now-happen-pc-83277.

Most of us operate in the yes-or-no real world. What many people don't understand is, in the digital world, *ignoring* is the new *no*. Let's say, hypothetically, that you send a message to someone you don't know hoping to persuade them to meet with you, and they ignore you (which obviously would never happen because you rock, but let's just go with it for the story's sake).

If your message fails to ignite any action, your message is ignored—it's not a yes and it's not a no—it's just a nothing. Your message didn't even register on their radar; they didn't even care enough to say no! I don't know about you, but that lack of reaction feels *worse* than a no. Rejecting you means at least they considered you. Ignoring you means you never even got up to bat. Every time someone scrolls past your message and ignores you, that's a no. It's not a "not yet." It's a no.

People say no (for the most part) to Foes and Sellers.

You might be thinking, *How can I possibly capture attention, stop the scroll, and inspire some kind of action from someone I've never met—someone behind a screen—in just two and a half seconds?*

Welcome to the reason I wrote this book. You'll learn the formula to accomplish exactly that—the same formula that

I've shared with global sales organizations across every vertical you can imagine: healthcare, technology, finance, real estate, even defense technology companies selling to the US government! You name it. This book will show you exactly how to successfully craft digital messaging that moves your recipients to take action—an open, a click, a reply, a meeting, a chance. You'll learn how to create messaging that moves them to do something besides scroll past and ignore. If you want to open opportunities, it's important to first persuade your recipient's brain that you are a Friend or a Server. Then, and only then, will they open your message. You'll also learn how to conduct less outreach for higher quality inbound leads. You'll learn how to exert less effort while scoring bigger wins. You'll learn how a personalized, quality-over-quantity approach will help you work smarter. You'll discover how to organically initiate stronger, more profitable relationships. You'll gain insights into how to design a professional life where you earn more meetings, drive more revenue, and realize more success, while eliminating rejection, increasing respectful relationships, eradicating unproductive efforts, and ultimately improving the overall quality of each day you're out there giving your all to make it happen.

My formula has helped countless people evolve their business development approach for the modern marketplace. A small shift in your outreach mindset will attract the responses you're looking for every time you type, text, or tweet. Whenever you touch your keyboard, you'll be messaging in ways that ultimately attract inbound opportunities. As entrepreneurs, sales pros, and managers, many of us have become conditioned to the idea that rejection is just "part of the gig." But rejection—a lack of being heard and respected—isn't fun. Every time your message doesn't warrant a response, every time you chase someone that doesn't want to engage with you, it drives your brain insane. It's a loose end, a loop you didn't close, a target you didn't hit. Internalizing those constant digital rejections will wear on you over time. Maybe not at first, but being ignored, being rejected, not garnering the responses you want—it's just not fun. More importantly, it's not necessary for sales success in our hyper-connected digital age.

You'll learn how just ten words can mean the difference between no responses and profitable relationships. You'll learn how improving one sentence can bring you success every time you touch your keyboard.

In working with more than one hundred of the world's biggest brands, I've helped optimize the success patterns that drive big results. In working intimately with their executives and stakeholders, I've been there to experience what works and what doesn't in the world of modern business development.

A BET AND A BOTTLE OF CAYMUS

When I started training some of these bigger organizations, I got a lot of pushback. In one instance, I was working with a large SEO firm and there was one guy in particular who was completely skeptical. Of course, he was their top producer and a little full of himself, as he'd already seen a lot of success relative to the rest of his team. He was convinced his LinkedIn messages were already ironclad perfection. I asked him if he would show me the messages he was sending. They were, in a word, *long*. They contained paragraph upon paragraph upon paragraph, almost all about himself, his company, his accomplishments, and how great they were at SEO/SEM and email marketing.

From this templated sales message, he was seeing a four-percent response rate, which he thought was awesome. And, compared to the one- to two-percent response rate of the other salespeople in the organization, it was.

Walking him through my formula, we rewrote a few of his messages together. I asked him to try this personalized, quality-over-quantity approach for one month. To raise the stakes, I bet him a hundred bucks that he'd widen the already-large lead he had on the rest of the sales team.

He took my bet. And by the end of the month, sure enough,

he'd increased his responses and widened his lead. (I took his hundred bucks in the form of a bottle of Caymus, but that's another story.)

He wasn't the only one who used my formula to craft more effective messages. The middle-of-the-pack reps moved closer to the top, and the ones who had been lagging saw some much-needed progress and gained new confidence.

Whether you're already a rock star, or you have some urgency to improve your current position; whether you're an entrepreneur who runs a successful business, but you're curious how you could achieve more; or whether you're in a sales support role and you're tasked with getting appointments on the calendar for your boss—this book is for you.

OPEN NEW OPPORTUNITIES

You have two and a half seconds, ten words, to inspire an action in a potential buyer. You have the amount of space in one message notification or an email preview before they scroll past your message and ignore you. In this book, you'll learn how to create smart, personal, and engaging messaging, so that your two and a half seconds count for as much as possible.

Most of your competitors are too set in their ways to read

a book like this. They're too focused on volume, and not focused enough on relationships. If anything, they're leaning *harder* into the copy, paste, repeat grind, and they're coming up very short.

By reading this book, you'll understand how to translate what works in person to what works in the digital space. There are proven, tested best practices in the following pages that will ignite real relationships. The best thing about this book is that once you implement what myself and so many others have, you'll create inbound opportunities and earn the respect and trust of your buyers. Can you imagine a world where not just a few, but *most*, of your potential buyers consider you a Friend? Can you imagine a world where your problem-solving has people's minds thinking of you gratefully as a business Server?

Every day, people are barely surviving a storm of templated digital hit-and-run messages from Foes and Sellers. Yours is the one that stops the scroll, pauses the swipe, and persuades a desired action.

With the same formula you'll learn in this book, I didn't just rebuild and explode my business. I didn't just sky-rocket my revenue and land dream clients overnight. I didn't just become an influencer in the world of digital sales and create a referral funnel that continues to grow my agency to this day. I built financial success, and more importantly, the multi-year relationships, referrals, and renewals that sustain and grow that success. I no longer have the pressure of outbound messaging. I haven't experienced in years that sinking feeling of, *Oh my God, I have to sell something—now—or else!*

But before I share with you my proven formula for becoming your most persuasive self, let's rewind a bit. The formula you'll learn in this book wasn't just born from working with the world's biggest brands. It was initially born from the purest success motivator there is: the need to survive.

STARTUP? TRY STARTDOWN

Have you ever been warned not to put all your eggs in one basket, but you ignored it because you thought you knew better?

Most classic startup stories begin at a kitchen table and end with a fancy office. My story starts in my kitchen, moves to an oceanfront palace, retreats back to my kitchen, moves to a modest office, back to my kitchen, and finally skyrockets into an international, lean, mean, remote-workforce machine. But I'm getting ahead of myself.

PARIS HILTON AND THE DOLLHOUSE

My social media agency, Socialite, began as a modest organization (of one) operating out of my house. It started when I was offered a job in San Francisco that I turned down. Instead, I offered to consult for them remotely from Orange County. Since I had never been a consultant, didn't really know what that entailed, and didn't have a consulting business—so when they accepted my offer, and asked what my company's name was, I panicked. They could *not* find out that they were my first consulting client and that I didn't actually have a consulting business, or I would lose the contract.

I was driving on the 405 from Los Angeles back to the OC when I got their call. "Our company name?" I stammered, trying to stall.

Frantically, I looked around and, at that exact moment, saw a billboard of Paris Hilton.

"Uh...Social...ite? Our company name is Socialite."

I held my breath until I heard them say, "Great—we'll mail payment to Socialite."

Later that day, I conducted the most terrifying GoDaddy and LLC searches of all time to see if the name was even available. Luckily, somehow, it was.

The Bay Area client referred me to another client, and then another. After two straight days of working in my pajamas and drinking Starbucks, I realized I couldn't remember when I'd last brushed my teeth. I needed help. But I didn't know where to look or how to hire someone.

Deciding I needed a break, I showered, brushed my teeth, and met my best friend Sheena out at a local music venue. In the bathroom line, I chatted with an adorable twenty-two-year-old brunette named Alexa who had just graduated college. She was telling me how she was looking for a job, and how her dad was threatening that if she didn't get one soon she would be in serious trouble. She seemed smart, hungry, and upbeat. Perfect. I told her upfront that I couldn't pay her and offered her an internship, thinking she wouldn't keep showing up to work for free. I also figured this was just bar talk, and I would probably never see this gal again. The next day, she knocked on my front door at 8:59 a.m.

She showed up the morning after that, and again the morning after that. Months later, she kept showing up at my house, so I had to start paying her. We worked side by side for nine hours a day, managing five clients' social media accounts. It was exhausting, but we were cranking out some excellent work. The referrals kept rolling in. I hired her best friend from New Jersey to join us at my small, round glass kitchen table. Suddenly, Socialite was a company.

At the time, I lived in a tiny seventies-style wood-paneled apartment in one of those former-daily-motel, dumpy apartment complexes. It was pretty outdated and smelled kind of grungy, but it was one block from the beach with a great view. We'd open the glass doors and a refreshing ocean breeze would blow in, clearing away all the decades of weirdos who had probably lived there before me.

One thing led to another, and we managed to land a *huge* financial services brand as our top client. (By huge, I mean you probably have one of their cards in your wallet.)

We popped the champagne, and before we'd even finished celebrating our giant win, I'd started looking for office space in prime oceanfront commercial real estate. We staffed up, and so began Socialite 2.0: new, improved, and with the revenue to grow!

One of my mentors, Megan, a sharp executive at of one of the largest insurance brands in the world, happened to live down the street. We'd go for beach walks and hikes, and I'd soak in every piece of advice she shared. When I told her about our big client the following morning, which was one of those blustery Laguna days—cloudy, off-season, deliciously gray—she congratulated me and was excited, but cautious. "That's great," she said. "That's a great win for you."

I could sense the warning in her tone. "Wait, what's wrong?" I asked her.

"No, really, I'm excited."

I knew she was hedging and asked again for the truth, this time a slight tinge of worry clouding the edges of my excitement. "Well, just—it sounds like a massive amount of your revenue is all from this one client," she explained.

While this mammoth client was more than seventy percent of our revenue, I reassured her (and myself) with a lot of bluster about the special relationship I had with the client. My contact at the company was a friend of a friend, someone I felt I had a great rapport with. The client loved my team, as we had helped save them from a few online reputation management crises, as well as dramatically improved their following and engagement on social media. We were a Friend-Server hybrid—the golden combination. They loved us. They'd never leave. Never. (Cue "crazy girl from *Wedding Crashers*" eyes.)

Like all great entrepreneurs, I had (and still have) what

many in my circles have described as a "delusional" level of confidence. I remember telling Megan, "They'll be our client for years. Nothing to worry about."

That was my first warning. The second came from another mentor of mine, the chairman of a huge OC real estate empire. When I met him for lunch a couple of weeks after the deal was struck, I tried to impress him by bragging about all the tens of thousands of dollars I was dropping to outfit our new oceanfront office with the complete contents of the Spring Pottery Barn catalog.

With the same faux-casual tone as my other mentor, he said, "You know, when we started, we found really good *used* furniture, for cheap."

Used? Was he kidding? Ew. Did he not know what a massive success I was? Where we were going? I dismissed his (in my mind) Goodwill suggestion and told him that, since we were going to hold client events at the office, everything had to be high-end to be "on brand."

It must have occurred to me somewhere in the back of my mind that two major tycoons had just given me the same warning: if seventy percent of our revenue came from this one client, that meant we'd *lose* seventy percent of our revenue if they ever decided to leave us. But I completely shut out that little voice in the back of my head telling me to heed the warnings. I was too pumped by success and too eager to keep growing faster; to do that, my agency needed to look the part.

We decked out our lavish oceanfront office with gorgeous décor and created a space perfect for hosting client events. My office theme was "all white everything"—white couches, white shag rug, pristine white desk, white leather rolling chair—basically, it was Pinterest perfection. We called it the Dollhouse.

Our success continued to blaze along. I did the classic new-success entrepreneur victory lap. I got one award after another; we threw huge events and got big-name bands down from LA to play at them. We were profiled in all the local business publications. We brought B-list Orange County celebs into the office all the time and blew through cash.

My ego got a little (okay, *a lot*) out of control, I'll admit. I wasn't listening to anyone, even though they were warning me of the same thing over and over: a critical amount of my revenue was sourced from one single client.

I felt secure in the fact that we were doing great work. We landed other decent-sized accounts, did an excellent job for them, and loved every second of it. I expanded the agency and carefully brought on the best social media experts I could find, and I soon had a huge team of hustlers working hard and surpassing all our goals. I really felt like I'd made it.

Until all those warnings I'd been ignoring came right back around to haunt me.

One deceptively beautiful Monday morning, sipping a cup of tea, I clicked open a short but devastating message. My point of contact at our biggest client had quit, and our account was now blowing in the wind and up for grabs. By Wednesday, we found out that our contract (written by our big client, who I hadn't wanted to piss off by making edits before signing) would not be renewed. By Friday, I suddenly faced the bleak prospect of having to rapidly slash all overhead just to make ends meet.

This is a gentler way of saying that I advanced final payroll on my personal credit card, laid off the majority of my incredible team, including one of my dearest friends—and if you've never fired a close friend, may you never experience that particular punch in the gut— and bounced on our lease. Faster than the crash of a Pacific Ocean wave, it was, "Later, oceanfront Pinterest heaven!"

The party was over. The Dollhouse shut down practically overnight. I had to put all the expensive Pottery Barn furniture—a small fortune in desks, couches, tables, rugs, and lamps—*somewhere*. So, I cleared all my own furniture out of my little apartment and put it in my tiny garage, and my apartment became the wood-paneled former motel room where Pottery Barn goes to die.

This is the point in the typical startup story where the main character cries herself to sleep over her huge failure and moves back in with her parents. And I definitely boo-hooed. A lot. However, in the middle of all the chaos and disappointment, something happened that would reinvent the way I earned new business and guide me to rebuild a stronger agency than the one I'd nearly lost.

The following Monday, the few employees I'd been able to afford to keep were crammed into my cramped, lavishly-furnished apartment like sardines. It was desk-touching-desk all throughout my living room. The huge glass conference table barely squeezed into what had formerly been my guest room. This was Socialite 3.0: scrappy, anxious, tiny, and in desperate need of new business to stay afloat. The remnants of my team started working on pouring attention on the remaining clients we had to make sure we kept them. It was my responsibility to find new clients to replace the big one we'd lost, and to say I was a little rusty in that department was an understatement. I was stressed, tired, heartsick, and a little desperate. Unless I could dig us up some big new clients, *and fast*, I was going to have to close up shop entirely and get a dreaded job. I remember being in the shower and seeing a huge clump of hair in my hand. I stopped getting my period and started having panic attacks. I had gone from chill surfer girl to manic stress ball overnight. The startup anxiety was starting to take me down.

If you've ever experienced the threat of failure on that scale, you know it is one powerful motivator. I was in pure survival mode. So, I decided to spray and pray.

All week, I copied and pasted the same sales message to hundreds of random people I found on LinkedIn:

Hi, XXXX—Let me take a moment to introduce myself. I'm Erin, the CEO/Founder of Socialite Agency.

(Side note: This is all that fit in the mobile notification, so just realize that I've already been ignored and sent to the inbox wasteland. My recipient didn't know me, they didn't care, and they scrolled by. In those two sentences, I referenced myself and my company five times! That's pretty much the best way NOT to persuade someone to read your message!)

We are the only social media agency in the world specializing strictly in social media management for large conferences, trade shows, and events. We help huge brands like VISA, Hitachi, Siemens, and others to amplify their events to the world using the power of social media marketing. Our clients realize increased attendance, brand awareness, and attendee engagement before, during, and especially after each of their events.

As CEO of Socialite, I respect your time and will be brief. Socialite's award-winning team of certified social media experts will take your event (or brand presence at an event) to the next level with a custom, measurable, targeted social media strategy. The event marketing world is taking notice as we have partnered with leaders like FreemanXP and others, plus been featured in Forbes, Business Insider, Yahoo, and PCMA magazine.

We have social media event management packages

starting at $20K. You can learn more about our services, packages, and pricing by visiting www.socialite.agency. You can also hear from current and past clients who have shared the results we have created for them using our tested, proprietary event social marketing formula.

STILL READING?

If you are, you're unlike the vast majority of people I sent this message out to.

Please let me know if you're available to chat tomorrow or Thursday afternoon around 10 a.m. PST. I'm looking forward to discussing how we can work together to help make your event or exhibit your most successful yet by harnessing the incredible power of social media.

Cheers!

Erin

Let me ask you: How many responses would you guess that message earned me in a week?

Maybe you're guessing one or two? Well, if you guessed zero, you're right.

I had Foe and/or Seller stamped all over me, worse than a terrible college spring break tattoo.

Maybe they could smell my desperation reeking in their inbox, but for some reason I didn't get a single response. I felt like a complete failure. My inbox wasn't empty. I had dozens of messages from friends and colleagues, wondering what had happened to The Dollhouse and whether we were still going to throw parties, but I had no responses from actual clients who would cut us checks. By Friday afternoon, all I could do was sit with my head in my hands, glaring at my stupid office-apartment—which now looked like an Apple Store stranded in the middle of a mountain hunting lodge, but at the beach (very confusing)—and come to the realization that the only *white* item I wanted at that moment was of the grape variety.

I dug out a bottle of Sauvignon Blanc, leftover from a client event we'd thrown just a few weeks ago when funding seemed endless, and poured it Chinese-restaurant-style all the way to the rim. I went back to my inbox, hoping upon hope that I'd see a response from a big fish just dying to sign a contract for Socialite to help them with a massive social media project.

I scrolled, scrolled, scrolled, and suddenly, three words popped out of the screen at me: *Hitachi Healthcare Caution.*

Hitachi Healthcare was, at the time, our second-biggest client. If anything happened to that account, we were going to go from working out of my tiny apartment to scouring job boards for a new plan. My brain immediately registered a Server, and I clicked open the message—*fast.*

> **Hitachi Healthcare Caution!**
>
> FYI, Facebook is making some API updates this weekend that could cause any scheduled client posts you have not to get published on time. Better check your settings.
>
> Dan

Is this guy for real? I thought. In a panic, I googled the supposed Facebook update, and sure enough, Dan was dead on. I quickly modified the settings on our social software program and dodged a huge bullet—we could *not* afford to mess up with any clients at that crisis moment! After correcting the mistake before it even happened, I breathed a sigh of relief. Would there ever be enough Savvy B in the world to make running a startup less stressful? Somewhat calmed, I turned my attention back to Dan. *Who is this mysterious Server?* After googling him, I found that he worked for a social media management software provider. I messaged him back.

Hitachi Healthcare Caution!

FYI, Facebook is making some API updates this weekend that could cause any scheduled client posts you have not to get published on time. Better check your settings.

Dan

Thanks for the heads up on that! Maybe we should be using you guys instead of our current platform. :)

He replied within a few minutes:

Hitachi Healthcare Caution!

FYI, Facebook is making some API updates this weekend that could cause any scheduled client posts you have not to get published on time. Better check your settings.

Dan

Thanks for the heads up on that! Maybe we should be using you guys instead of our current platform. :)

Maybe you should. :)

Maybe we could talk about it next week. Maybe Wednesday, 11am?

I gave him my number, put the meeting on my calendar, and went back to brooding over my current dire situation. My head swam with thoughts of my name in the OC papers, the champagne-fueled rock star parties, and how far I'd suddenly fallen—as if the last few years hadn't even happened. Why hadn't anyone responded to my outreach all week? What was I going to do? The Sauvignon Blanc was disappearing fast, and I was no closer to a solution.

Wait a minute.

It suddenly hit me that I'd just had the very interaction with Dan I was hoping for in my own inbox. I'd responded to his message! And he'd successfully set up a sales meeting with me, his prospect! Had he just digitally persuaded me? How had he been able to do it when I hadn't been able to get anyone to respond to *my* outreach?

My brain had decided to categorize Dan's message as a Server.

Intrigued, I stared at the sales message I'd been sending out all week. Then I stared at Dan's message. His *two sentences* had been more successful than my multiple *paragraphs*. Not only had he digitally persuaded me to meet with him, but this digital sales ninja had done it in *two sentences!*

That night, over the rest of the Sauvignon Blanc, I dug through my inbox searching for cold messages I'd responded to in the past. All in all, I scoured through over one thousand messages. My mini-research project yielded the following:

- Of one thousand inbound messages, I'd only responded to twenty. That's a two percent response rate. (Standard, right?)
- Of that two percent, I'd agreed to meet with sixty-five percent of those sales professionals. (Skype, phone, in-person meetings.)
- Of those meetings, I signed a purchase agreement with forty percent of them.

Out of one thousand messages, I'd been persuaded to buy from a mere five vendors. But of the messages I'd responded to, a quarter of them had been able to close the deal.

DO THE MATH

What's your send-to-open ratio? Your open-to-response ratio? Carve out a couple of hours to figure out how your messages are performing. It'll be the best few hours you spend on your business all year.

Flipping around to the other side of the table, it became

clear to me that if I could get my messages read, I'd have a pretty great shot at closing. It was also clear that the "perfect" sales message I'd crafted and sent out that week to drum up desperately-needed new business probably wasn't even getting *read*, let alone considered. I was a Seller to some, probably a Foe to most.

I re-read every successful message I'd responded to. Why had those messages worked and mine hadn't? How had these people persuaded me to respond, while my own messages got crickets? Was there a pattern to these successful messages? Was it something I could do too?

Turns out, the answer was *yes*. Once I figured it out, honed it into a formula, and started using that formula to rebuild my business, my agency came roaring back to life.

This doesn't mean I got to head back to the Riviera office just yet. My team kept our remaining small fish happy, while I focused on this new way of messaging. I was determined to be a Friend or Server to as many leads as I possibly could. I cut my message volume by a huge percentage and focused my attention on researching the heck out of every single potential prospect. And it worked. It worked *incredibly well*. Instead of one hundred emails a day and a few responses, I was sending out around ten emails a day—and six or seven would inspire an action.

Sometimes that action was an open. Sometimes it was a profile view. Sometimes it was a click to our website. Sometimes it was a response, which led to a meeting, to a deal, to a referral, to another client, to repeat clients—and from there, Socialite Agency thundered back to life as Socialite 3.0.

In the days of The Dollhouse, most of our clients had been local brands, and we'd considered ourselves successful. With a combination of reworking our model to be more scalable and industry-specific, and this new method of digitally persuasive outreach, our client base quickly became *national and global*. Talk about the big leagues. It completely changed the face of our business and the trajectory of my career. I went from losing friends, losing face, and losing confidence, to signing clients like the Oscars and ABC/Disney—even Nelson Mandela's family hired us to run social media for his ninety-fifth birthday celebration in Manhattan.

The approach to persuasive digital outreach you'll learn in this book isn't just "social selling." I don't love the term *social selling*, because what works about this approach is that you actually aren't selling at all. You're focusing on digital personalization to persuade someone to hear you, consider you, and organically start a new relationship with you and your company.

In the digital age, the hard sell is dead. People don't want Sellers, and they love deleting Foes. It just doesn't work like it used to. It's time to ditch the pitch and get personal. Digital persuasion success is custom. It's creative. It's relationship-driven. It's anti-automation and anti-selling. And, using my formula, it's fairly easy to do.

I don't believe that, in this day and age, you can hard sell anyone anything. What you *can* do is persuade someone to give you a chance to engage, check you out, and start a relationship using just your words from behind the screen.

In this book, you'll learn how to embrace a new mindset and mentality that will drive better relationships that lead to greater opportunities. This is more than a formula; it's a modernized approach for the future of business development in the digital age.

The best part of this strategy is that it's proven. I speak on this topic frequently, and not an event goes by where I don't get messages from people in my audiences saying what they tried, how it worked, and how excited they were! The formula you'll learn in this book has worked so well for both Socialite and my speaking business that I rarely have a need to do outbound digital business development. Now, most of my clients come to me through referrals and word of mouth.

Many of my Socialite clients, after we help with their social media, ask my team and I to train their sales organizations to become Friends and Servers. The success I've experienced so far has happened by being authentic, getting personal, and maximizing the engagement potential of every single messaging outreach. You can replicate this for yourself and, when you do, you'll see your revenue and success skyrocket, just like I did. It's worked for me as an entrepreneur, it's worked for the global sales organizations who hired me to teach them my formula, and it will work for you.

WHO HAS TIME FOR THIS?

You're probably thinking what a lot of my clients say after I share my formula for digitally persuasive messaging outreach: *I don't have time for this. I have enough Friends. And I'm sure as heck not a Server.*

Most people in my audiences and workshops initially say the same thing. I'll never forget one particularly special moment when I was onstage in front of three hundred project management software sales representatives in Chicago. I had finished my presentation and was conducting the question and answer portion of my program. One tall, older Italian gentleman raised his hand and said, "Uh, yeah. I have a question. What if you hate social media, and what if you don't have time for all this stupid crap?" In the moment, I resisted the urge to cheekily correct him on actually having two questions and bit my lip. It was tough being put on the spot, and I tried my best to explain. Like most things in life, it's typically more effective to show, not tell. So, I showed them.

After six months of working with this team, the same fellow came up to me one afternoon and told me that, even though he initially thought it was a waste of time, he was now ranked in the top five percent of the company— for the first time in fifteen years. He shook my hand and humbly thanked me profusely, which more than made up for his aggressive questioning months before. Another member of the same team said that once she calculated the time that she ultimately saved overall by building a constant stream of lucrative relationships, she couldn't believe she'd ever approached new business development any other way.

"Why isn't everyone doing this?" she asked incredulously.

"I don't know," I answered, "but they're going to catch on sooner or later, so just enjoy your first-mover advantage while you can!"

Have you ever said you don't have time for something but,

deep down, you know it simply means it's not a priority for you? Not "having time" simply means prioritizing something else *in place* of what we claim we don't have time for. You don't have time to go to the gym—or do you, and just don't feel like it? You don't have time to have drinks with that friend who keeps texting you—or are you really just not that interested in maintaining the friendship?

We don't want to try new methods because they're either hard, they're unfamiliar, or we can't be sure of the return on our efforts. I get that. I know that in our crazy-busy, slammed, always-be-closing grind, it seems like there couldn't possibly be time to do effective research on every single prospect. How can you hit your target of one hundred new outreach messages a day if each one takes a half hour?

OLD-SCHOOL METHODS IN A SOCIAL AND DIGITAL WORLD

Deliberately or not, we all choose how we spend our time. Spending time on typical spray-and-pray sales outreach, traditional numbers-game sales formulas, and digital hit-and-runs—the equivalent of smiling-and-dialing online—are remnants of the pre-internet era. Before Google and social media, you *had* to reach out to a hundred people and ask them if they were interested in your product or service, because how else were you supposed to find out? When we continue this numbers game, this rinse-and-repeat formula, we completely ignore the money-making, time-saving tools of social and digital networks.

Are you digitally dialing for dollars?

In global sales organizations I've trained, when more quality time is spent per prospect, less time is wasted overall, and the overall return on that time investment is consistently higher. Sales has moved from top-down communication—copy that's created by marketing, put into an executive-approved template, and sent to all the sales reps on the team to digitally hammer prospects with—to *network* communication. Researching potential connections and building real relationships is the future of business success in the modern marketplace. *As mobile, social, and digitally-empowered consumers, we're looking to company representatives, not for authority and education, but for friendship and problem solving.* This is the great business communication shift of our time, and it's just happened in the last few years. Luckily for you, you have a small window to take advantage of this before everyone else catches on.

Think of a typical day in your life as a sales professional or entrepreneur. We all have different ways of approaching it. Maybe you get up early, work out, then grab a huge cup of coffee and sit down at your desk. You fire up your computer and open your inbox. After you tackle the most pressing items, you move on to the bulk of your work: cold outreach. Finding people who will say *yes*.

Now what do you do? Do you just open up your CRM and start knocking through names? Do you start auto-sending messages and begin your day with a series of digital hit-and-runs?

Maybe you have some kind of sales message template you use. Whether you created it or it was passed down by your marketing team, it probably goes something like this:

Hi, Name,

This is who I am. This is why I rock. Here's what our

group does that rocks. Here's who else thinks we rock. It's going to take you three more thumb swipes to scroll through of all of our rocking offerings. Can I meet with you to tell you more about why we rock and why you should hire us so you can rock too?

Maybe this looks familiar to you? Of course, you would never *send* a generic message like this, but maybe you've received one.

WHICH ONE ARE THEY?

Would you scroll, swipe, or read?

What happens way too often is that someone will open up a template, which at this point is generic enough—for the sake of efficiency—that they won't even tweak it. They copy-paste it into emails, LinkedIn messages, tweets, Facebook messaging, and other platforms. Copy, paste, repeat. Copy, paste, repeat. Sometimes they do this hundreds of times and it becomes a blur. Hours later, maybe they've hit their target of fifty or one hundred messages, and their coffee is sitting cold on the desk beside them, forgotten. Of course, this isn't you, but let's just say that, hypothetically, you can relate to this scenario just a smidge.

Are you using your cold outreach messages as what are essentially digital cold calls? Maybe this is your approach; maybe it's not. If it *is* your approach, do you believe that it's really a good use of your time? More than that, is it the *best* use of your time?

If you're reading this book, you're obviously a bright, hard-working go-getter. You're a relationship-builder. An opportunity-opener. A closer. A make-shit-happen kind of personality. And I like that about you. A lot. I respect the hustle in all forms, but let's be real: don't you think endlessly copy-pasting the same generic sales message over and over again is kind of...beneath you? Do you really want to be classified as a Foe or Seller? I don't!

Continuing with this obviously-hypothetical scenario, was your return on that time overwhelmingly successful? Did this approach net you a handful of responses? Out of a full day of copy-pasting? If that feels acceptable to you and you're comfortable with it, definitely keep doing it. Crank up the Spotify, chill, copy-paste to your heart's content, and net your one- to three-percent response rate. If that works for you, there's nothing wrong with that. Do what you do! Feel free to torch this book or use it as a doorstop.

But, if you're like me and a lot of the sales pros I work with, and you don't feel a ninety-seven- to ninety-nine-percent rejection rate should be considered a winning strategy, then keep reading. As an entrepreneur, I want to spend my time on my client relationships and on making sure I'm delivering dynamic results from work that matters. I also cherish precious time with my husband, family, friends, and colleagues. I want to spend time surfing, snowboarding, hiking, biking, golfing, playing tennis, traveling, reading, playing guitar—yes, I love all of these things! But they take time, and I would much rather spend time with the people I love, doing the things I love, than stuck in some "well that's just the way it's always been done" business development mentality. I also don't want my name and my reputation associated with annoying people. I don't want to waste my time or waste the time of my prospects. I want to use the incredible digital tools available to me to work smarter, not harder in this exciting modern marketplace. I want to win more business while minimizing my rejection and buyer annoyance. Don't you?

Well, we're not the only ones.

I've helped companies like Hitachi, VISA, Siemens, ABC/Disney, AEG, Abbott Laboratories, and Synchrony Financial better leverage their digital communications to win on a global scale. They've experienced lower message volume with greater depth of relationships, which led to increased sales, referrals, up-sells, and cross-sells. I've experienced building my business from a dumpy kitchen table to the red carpets of Hollywood, from two people working in our pajamas to an international, award-winning agency. And we're not alone. There are dozens of other industry leaders winning big by evolving their sales strategy for the digital age. Here are a few notable highlights:[7]

- When IBM started using a social selling approach similar to my formula, they increased sales by 400 percent.
- InContact deployed a personalized sales approach and increased their revenue per sale by 122 percent.
- SAP claims that developing this personalized, researched approach to sales outreach online delivered thirty-two percent more revenue, and they were ten percent more likely to achieve quota.
- Log My Calls shared helpful personalized content with prospects instead of using a standard canned sales template and saw a 400 percent increase in leads in ninety days.
- Sprint worked with Sales for Life (they use a similar approach to my formula) to dramatically increase opportunities and deals company-wide in just ten weeks.

---

7   Stephen Walsh, "6 Case Studies of Social Selling Success," Anders Pink, accessed September 4, 2017, http://blog.anderspink. com/2017/05/6-case-studies-of-social-selling-success/.

The art of digital persuasion is more than social selling, and it's more than just a long-term sales strategy. It's an investment that pays off exponentially in the future. This kind of personalized method sounds like a significant time investment, but, in the long run, it will *save* you time and even more frustration. If you want to stand out and avoid the inbox wasteland, this type of approach is quickly becoming the only smart, viable option.

The classic sales script—kind of like the typical sales message—is what's usually used by senders to most targets. If you're sending a general version of that same message, you're completely blending in. You're not standing out. You're not being heard. You're making it harder on yourself to truly succeed. People seek Friends and Servers, and they avoid Foes and Sellers like a vegan avoids a burger joint.

An incredibly successful messaging makeover does take a little work and a little creativity—but, like all good things in life, it's worth working at.

Imagine a whole different scenario for your workday. Here's the scenario that I've experienced and my clients have responded to. It's a scenario that hundreds of the sales reps I've worked with have experienced. This is what you can expect. Envision this as your new sales reality:

You wake up in the morning refreshed from the previous day's success. You work out, grab a coffee, and sit down at your desk. You fire up your laptop to find dozens of responses in your inbox. You take a couple hours to follow up on those—and each one is a true connection with the person on the other end, a real conversation. Then you move on to your messages. You'll send out ten today, maybe twenty—it depends on how much quality information you have on good relationship prospects you've already identified and who might at some point want (or know someone who wants) your product or service. You begin composing creative, personalized messages to your prospects, inspiring them to take action with each persuasive outreach. As you're sending these messages, your inbox already begins to ding with replies. You see lots of new views on your profile. You see that your opens are at an all-time high. You end the day feeling satisfied. Not only are you *not* associating yourself with the legions of sales scripts, and not only are you opening opportunities for deep, real relationships, but you actually see your calendar filling up with a greater number of meetings. You see far fewer rejections and spend much less time on copy-paste waste. *You're a Friend. You're a Server.*

THE ART OF DIGITAL PERSUASION

If you've been reading this and thinking to yourself:

This sounds great, but how can I really engage someone in ten words?

What would I possibly write?

How can I persuade someone to give me a chance in the space of a message notification or inbox preview?

These are the types of responses I get in my workshops *before* deploying my formula.

After my formula, my workshop attendees see that just changing one sentence in their approach is the difference between being answered and being ignored.

You have everything to gain from learning the art of digital persuasion. Most sales professionals haven't adapted their outreach to the digital age. They're not thinking in terms of the one-sentence hook. They're not thinking about having only two and a half seconds or ten words to get read. They're being ignored.

I've never gone back to the desperation of my apartment crammed with overpriced office furniture, to staring at an inbox full of junk mail, but not a single reply from a potential buyer. Or to feeling that ping of my sales conscience, where I know that what I'm doing is ineffective and maybe even impolite or inappropriate, but I feel like I don't have a choice. Or to feeling I'm sending things I'm not proud of, messages I wouldn't send to a friend of a friend. I've gained the lightness and freedom of deep relationships and inbound deals, without the heavy feeling of being *that* salesperson. Have you ever had that feeling?

I learned how to improve the way I communicate with everyone, every day. I came away from conversations satisfied and charged up for the next one. I cut the stress and gained connections—and had way more time to enjoy nature and expand the depth of those connections.

I'm so grateful for how this formula has helped me save my business, save my sanity, and supercharge my life. I'm so grateful that it's helped so many sales professionals and teams around the world. And now, I'm so grateful and happy to share it with you, so that you can experience the same results in your life.

THE DAY THE COFFEE RAN OUT

Do you remember the first day of your first adult job?

Mine was on a cloudy grey Monday morning in Baltimore
City, Maryland. I'd been a college graduate for less than
forty-eight hours when I pulled up to the local TV station
with no idea what to expect. I'd heeded the advice my dad
gave me, which was, "Who cares what you're passionate
about? Just get a *job* before you graduate. Preferably in
sales so you'll always be able to make money." So, I did.
The station had hired me over the phone for a commis-
sioned sales position. At the time, the advice had seemed
a little harsh, but looking back, as usual, my dad was right.

The outdated, unfriendly brick building was not exactly the glamorous environment I had pictured (or described boastfully to my friends). I'd had to double-check my MapQuest printout twice to make sure I was in the right place! The receptionist looked like a hung-over librarian, and the lobby had the faintest hint of cigarette smoke, probably left over from the seventies. Walking past the TV news desks and shouting camera crews, it was clear pretty quickly that this place was less Hollywood and more like *The Wire* meets *Anchorman*. Feeling suddenly very nervous, I reported to my new boss's office for training. I summoned up every shred of confidence and poise I had, opened my new boss's door, and immediately locked eyes with Alec Baldwin.

Depending on how old you are, you might be, like me, a product of the ABC (Always Be Closing) generation. If you've been working in sales for more than fifteen years, you've probably seen *Glengarry Glen Ross,* right? If you have, picture that movie's biggest fan of all time, and it was my new boss. He was a fast-talking, coffee-slugging Jewish guy from Queens with a life-size cardboard cutout of Alec Baldwin standing next to his desk.

I sat down in front of his desk, which was covered with New York Yankees tchotchkes—we were in Orioles country—and a huge coffee mug printed with "COFFEE'S FOR

CLOSERS." He took out the Baltimore City Yellow Pages and slammed it down on the desk in front of me.

"Welcome to the number one TV news station in Baltimore! Well, depending on who you talk to. Do you know what these are?"

He slid a printout with a million tiny numbers in columns across his desk.

Timidly, I replied: "Um, no, sorry, I don't."

"These are Nielsen ratings. These are *very, very* important. You check these first thing every morning," he said.

Taking a huge slug of coffee, he eyed me like a hawk.

"Have you ever sold anything before?"

Guessing that selling tickets to our last raging keg party in College Park didn't count, I admitted, "No."

"Okay. Here's how it works. You open this book. You call one hundred businesses a day. You ask if someone will meet with you to learn about how advertising on our television station can help grow their business. Ten of those one hundred people will agree to let you come by for a meeting. You drive to their office. You ask them questions about their business. You shut up and you *listen*. You ask for a second appointment to bring back a proposal. Five of those ten will let you come back to present this PowerPoint with our rates."

He slammed down a huge, old-school PowerPoint deck printout.

"Our rates are in here. Are our rates negotiable? *No.* If they are going to sign a contract that day though, the answer is yes."

"Okay—"

You try to convince as many as you can to sign this contract. If you're any good, maybe one of them will close about once a month. You get to keep twenty percent commission on each contract signed. It only counts if you *bring me the deposit check to produce their commercial.* Any questions?"

I opened my mouth to volley about a hundred at him, and he cut me off. "Good. Go get 'em."

That was it; the full extent of my "training." I went back to my desk, opened the phone book to the A's, and started dialing—keenly aware of all the other seasoned sales reps in that cubicle hell snickering at the fresh meat on her first day. I called A1 Plumbing and was immediately hung up on.

Great. On to the next.

After being hung up on by A1 Plumbing, A1 Chinese, A1 Auto Body, and A1 Lawn Care, I hadn't accomplished much besides sending my pride and my confidence into the gutter.

Feeling frustrated and like I should just quit on my first day—and dreaming about my recent responsibility-free days of college—I started doing the math: how long till I could retire? Did I really have to endure forty more years of this?

A woman named Kim sashayed up to my desk. Kim was a beautiful, tan, blonde dynamo who looked like Heather Locklear. She was wearing the same Express power suit and fancy pointy pumps that was the Ally McBeal-style uniform back then, plus a huge diamond ring. My Target work outfit that I'd felt so confident about earlier that morning suddenly looked like a dishrag in comparison.

"First days are tough. How 'bout I take you to lunch?" she asked me, sliding on her Chanel sunglasses and ushering me out to her silver BMW.

Over lunch, Kim explained that, when cold calling people, there were many components to success: your tone of voice, establishing rapport with the receptionist, and the importance of your opening sentence. She gave me an example: "Good morning, Claire, how are you? Thank goodness it's Friday, huh? This is Kim with FOX45 TV in Baltimore, and I have something exciting to share with your marketing director if they are around at the moment please?" She then went on, "You want to sound important, while also becoming their friend. They are called the gatekeepers, and you want to sweet talk them into opening that gate."

Over my first hundred or so calls that first week, I began to learn how to persuade people to meet with me. The tiniest nuances—how high or low my voice was, smiling or serious, whether I was sitting or standing, whether I talked fast or slow—all of these affected whether someone hung up on me or agreed to a meeting.

Do you remember the day you closed your first deal? Of course you do! I'll never forget mine:

That Friday morning, Amos, from Amos's Pennsylvania Amish Homemade Furniture Market, agreed to meet with me. Kim was kind enough to take me on my first appointment in her fancy car, since my mom's hand-me-down minivan didn't exactly scream success. Amos didn't even own a TV, but he listened attentively as Kim smoothly presented a plan for him to buy $10,000 worth of TV ads, so he could showcase his beautiful picnic tables and pergolas to the whole state of Maryland. Currently, he was only attracting customers who happened to drive by and see his sign from the side of the not-very-busy road. Kim was offering a solution that, to a struggling local business, may have been perceived as a Server. When she was finished, he stroked his long bushy beard thoughtfully and looked at me. I hadn't said one word the entire meeting, just turned the pages of the PowerPoint for Kim when she gave me the nod.

"Well what do *you* think?" Amos asked me.

Without thinking, I looked right into his eyes and said as confidently as I could: "I think you should do it." There was a pause that felt like an eternity, and to my utter shock and disbelief, Amos picked up the pen Kim had laid out and signed the contract right then and there.

In that moment, I felt for the first time that indescribable rush of excitement that you can only get from closing a deal. I had found my calling, and it was now time for a cup of coffee.

My first commission checks started to roll in. I graduated

from ramen to restaurants, and soon I had a fancy car just like Kim. Within months, I was ranked second (after Kim, of course) not just for our local station, but out of all thirty-six stations the broadcast group owned in the country. I shattered previous business records using a combination of cold calls, in-person PowerPoint presentations, and taking people to sporting events and lunches all around Baltimore. Car dealerships, dentists, realtors, lawyers, you name it! It was 2004, and everyone wanted to grow their business using the power of television.

If this story sounds familiar to you, then you know that while this all sounds highly professional and methodical, between you and me, I was really just wearing people down until they begrudgingly signed a contract just so I'd leave them alone. I would call back, leave voicemails, stop by because I happened to "be in the neighborhood." I brought enough donuts to give the entire company diabetes. I stalked and I hounded! I'm sure you have *never* done anything like that, right?

After a few years as a rising ad sales superstar, Kim and I were both recruited to join a Baltimore startup that had invented a matching software for early social selling—a LinkedIn-type networking platform for trade shows and conferences, before LinkedIn had taken off. When I graduated from my little local TV station to the big leagues, I was suddenly dealing with huge national brands like LG, Panasonic, and Black and Decker. I was all of twenty-four, and my whole job was explaining the concept of people connecting and networking online before social media had become what it is today. I flew to Vegas, Orlando, Chicago, and San Francisco constantly for trade shows; I had an expense account and all the resources I needed to wine and dine big clients into buying our software to connect with buyers before trade shows and expos.

Getting these huge national brands to meet with me was a little more complicated than getting a meeting with Amos from Amos's Pennsylvania Amish Homemade Furniture Market. I began learning the nuances of these new circles of the more polished global sales professionals. Even though it was more challenging to get in front of people and get them to agree to meet with me, sending emails and calling them was still the way to do it. Usually it took three or four calls to get a meeting on the books, or two or three emails to get a response. Back in 2006, these messages still worked.

In 2007, when social media still wasn't mainstream, it took an average of 3.68 cold call attempts to reach a prospect. Today, it takes an average of eight attempts. Fewer than one percent of cold calls now result in appointments. In other words, it takes about three times as much effort to land one qualified appointment now as it did in 2007. A lot has changed in just ten years.

It wasn't until 2008, when I launched my first company—a website development firm called Jump Digital Media launched with my friend Danielle—that I really noticed the game was changing. Then, a few years later, I realized that social media, not custom website development, was the next digital marketing frontier. The game had changed completely. Suddenly, anyone in business development was working three times as hard for the same number of opportunities. Actually, that's not quite true—*many* people still worked the same amount, but only closed a third of the business they were used to. Those of us who leaned harder into the grind quickly grew frustrated. Let's be honest: it *sucks* working three times as hard and not seeing three times the profit.

The coffee had run out. The game had changed, and most of the players either weren't aware or had no idea how to evolve with the new rules.

I was lucky. I recognized the change quickly and pivoted fast enough to fill a new niche. When Socialite started to grow in 2012, I suddenly found myself occupying all three seats at the deal table: pushy sales professional, corporate marketer, and finally, CEO.

It was at this moment that I truly understood the concept of karma.

RESEARCH IS THE NEW LISTENING

The minute I changed my LinkedIn profile to Founder/CEO, I was (and still am!) hounded by messages at every hour of the day. Emails, tweets, social media notifications, voicemails, you name it. Most reps wanted me to purchase everything from software to insurance to accounting. One even cold called me and left a three-minute message on my voicemail—*asking me to purchase cold calling services.* My LinkedIn and email inboxes were overflowing with paragraph after paragraph of horrendous, self-centered sales pitches from Foes and Sellers alike.

I'd get emails from sales professionals that were four to six paragraphs using—you guessed it—the classic script. *This is me, this is my company, this is what we do, can I get time on your calendar?* I'd get cryptic messages from sellers who didn't even describe or mention the product or service they were trying to sell me, and just wanted to "pick my brain" for "mutual crossover," whatever that means. I'd get weird passive-aggressive emails—*I guess since you haven't responded to my emails, you really don't want to be a leader in your industry, so this is the last time you'll hear from me.*

Mostly, though, what I'd get was the same email over and over again. It was almost like a template, and it hasn't changed much in the years since. It started with the word *I*.

Hi, Erin, I'm reaching out because I thought you might be interested in...

I'm just writing to see if you'd be interested in hearing about an amazing opportunity...

I represent an enterprise mobility and web development company...

I'm looking forward to getting to know you better. What's your core business?

I, I, I. The majority of messages always started from a self-centered place, focused on the *Seller* with the words *I, we, my,* or *us*. If their aim was to stand out and get my attention, they were going about it all the wrong way. It got to a point where, if I didn't recognize the sender or saw the word "I" in the email preview, I couldn't bring myself to open it. And that's where my troubled relationship with my inbox began.

I-MESSAGES

After the general greeting, how many of the messages you receive start with the word "I"? Start to notice this "I" epidemic, and you'll want to start deleting it in your own messages.

You can understand the annoyance, right? What's more annoying than uninspiring, me-focused digital messaging, in all forms? Part of this annoyance was born from the fact that these sales professionals—with their endless, cold, impersonal, botched messaging—reminded me of my days of cold calling the phone book, and it wasn't a flattering reflection.

Have you ever received messages like these in your own inboxes? Whether we want to admit it or not, the cold-call method that worked so well in the old days has seriously lost its effectiveness. Our brains have evolved now to know better. It's digital Darwinism.

As with most things in life, there's always the one-percent exception, though. On rare occasions, there's a message on my phone that, for whatever reason, may move me to action. Although extremely few and far between, some messages stand out in my inbox and stop my scroll. The first few words inspire me to do something besides ignore them.

Meredith Adkins thought we should connect.

Baltimore Ravens fan?

Laguna Beach? Love that place!

Maryland grad? Go Terps!

Jackson Hole is so epic!

Each message caught my eye because it led with something highly personal and specific about me and my life—right from the first word. These messages had my brain registering the sender as a potential Friend.

Friends know you. Sellers don't.

With just one or two words, the implied message is, "I took time to research who you are and what you're about. I am not like every other salesperson." The personalization of someone, someplace, something that is highly personal to me instinctively persuaded me to stop scrolling and start reading. With this custom approach, from the first word, the person on the other end of this message quite literally put me—*not them*—first. They opened with proper, specific nouns from my past—places I'd lived, hobbies I'd had, people I knew. They referenced mutual friends. The sender had obviously taken the time to learn about me, learn about what I liked, who I was, and what was important to me. What's more engaging that that?

These smart senders understood that the goal of an introductory message was not to educate me or solve my deepest needs, but just to naturally engage me in an appropriate way that was personal to me. Their aim was to ignite an organic, natural start to what might blossom into a real relationship. The type of language they were using showed that I was a person, not a prospect. Their goal was to get my attention and persuade me to take action—check out their profile, respond, engage in short banter, anything but ignore them as just another sales message. By treating me as a person, I instinctively reciprocated with the respect of treating them as one. The people who treated me like a prospect were naturally treated as salespeople. Smart senders understood that the goal of a first-touch digital outreach was simply to politely open a mutually beneficial dialogue.

It's similar to the dating world. Can you imagine asking someone to marry you after two drinks? No way. You proceed with caution and explore whether the relationship might be a good fit for both of you. In the online dating world, you don't ask someone out right away—you wait until you've gone back and forth and established a digital connection. That's why it's shocking that ninety-eight percent of the messages I receive are people introducing themselves, talking about themselves, and asking for a meeting—all in the same first message! *Too. Freaking. Soon.*

These messages from not-so-smart senders go on and on, as if I'd reached out to them first and said, "Tell me about yourself." Which is not what had happened. At all.

If you want to master the art of becoming a more persuasive digital communicator, begin with translating the most important skill every great sales professional has for the online environment. The world's best sales professionals are always the best *listeners*.

> In the digital space, the world's best sales professionals are expert researchers. Researching someone online is the digital equivalent of listening. Great googlers and LinkedIn observers are the most persuasive people when messaging from behind the screen.

Research is the new listening. It's searching for clues to answer specific questions: *What does my prospect need? What does my prospect care about?* Not, *What do I need from my prospect? What can I sell my prospect? How can I convince my prospect?*

We all get so many messages, and have so little time. When you, as a sales rep, take the time to research someone, you're giving someone the same gift as when you actively listen to them. Taking the time to look up your prospect connects you to them. So much of the modern marketplace is about scale—this prompts automation. Automation is fantastic for marketing messaging. For sales, though, automation is not optimally persuasive. Automating relationships in our hyper-networked business world is like paying a bunch of people to go around to all the bars for you with a script to recite to every attractive person they see to try to find you a romantic partner. Not going to work. At least, not on the type of person with whom you want to spend quality time engaging.

If you want to stand out, taking that time in your day and spending it getting to know a digital prospect shows that prospect that you care about them as a person. It demonstrates your genuine interest. It creates the same feeling as actively listening to your prospect face to face. It makes them feel special. It makes them *like* you. Liking is one of the most powerful, persuasive feelings you can inspire. It inspires your digital prospect to action because it positively appeals to ego.

Without research, without personalization, that feeling doesn't happen. The lack of research signals indifference. It signals that they're the same as every other prospect you're reaching out to. They don't get an inspired feeling; they feel like another figure in a faceless crowd.

When they feel nothing, they do nothing.

Think about the last time you were invited to something on a huge generic group text message. How did that make you feel? Special? Probably not.

It's shocking to me how many times I'll agree to meet with someone and they'll default to the classic sales discovery questions—the same questions I learned to ask back in the early 2000s, before everyone was on social media!

Tell me about your business.

What are your challenges?

Who are your clients and competitors?

What is your unique value proposition?

What are some of your business goals?

Are you serious?! It's a horrible position to be in from the buyer's side of the table, because that unprepared seller just forced me to act like a jerk and as politely as possible ask them to please leave. *Why?!* There is no excuse to ever attend any meeting unprepared, without your prospect's career history, and what you think are probably the best answers to those questions.

The most persuasive phrase you can open with on a call or in a meeting in the age of digital is this:

In researching you and your company, it seems that xyz; is that accurate?

Boom. I'm in and I'm interested.

IS IT GOOGLEABLE?

Why ask a prospect anything you can find out on your own? The most successful social sales pros are the ones who anticipate questions and research answers and insights ahead of time. Doing this shows the prospect that you care about them, that they matter to you. It's also flattering, because you've taken the time to check out who they are. Spending your precious time on them speaks volumes that no fancy marketing materials, slick product knowledge, or witty banter can ever compete with.

Think about the last time you met someone at a cocktail party. You introduce yourself and the person responds, "Oh, yeah, Erin! I heard about you, and I looked up your profile—that article you wrote was great!" It feels awesome, right? Almost like talking to a friend who already knows you.

That's the feeling you want to inspire. You want to move them to a positive emotion that will ultimately open an opportunity.

Digital persuasion is part art, part science. It blends the science of psychology with the art of creative language. The *art* is how you use language, how you come up with a creative approach to move from *self*-focused, to *prospective*-focused. Friends care about you. Sellers don't.

Anytime you go to your keyboard or phone, the more you get into the habit and mindset of being *others*-aware, rather than *self*-aware, your opportunities will explode on a larger, wider, deeper scale than you could ever imagine. You'll start to make the same connections that you so easily make in real life, but on the scale and scope that was hard to achieve prior to the rise of digital.

For the last couple of decades, this concept of becoming more self-aware consumed us. Whether you're a sales professional or an entrepreneur, many of us have engaged in some form of self-discovery. Have you ever taken a Myers-Briggs test? A StrengthsFinder evaluation? A Facebook quiz? We exist in a hyper-narcissistic selfie society, and there's nothing we love more than contemplating who we are and what makes us special. I get it—it's way more fun and way easier to think about ourselves than to think about others! That's why I ask my workshop attendees to categorize themselves, not just in their own eyes, but in the eyes of *others*. How does your *recipient's* brain perceive you?

Friend?

Foe?

Seller?

Server?

It's definitely important to know your strengths and what makes you unique; you can use your special skillsets to improve and succeed. But in our endless quest to be so self-aware, have we forgotten to spend enough time, energy, or creativity on being others-aware before we reach out? How do you uncover what matters to someone else? How do you discover what they care about? How can you put yourself in the shoes of someone you've never met? Well, luckily, in the modern business era, it's pretty darn easy with a little effort and creativity! Once you have them, it's fairly easy to lead with those proposed insights when you reach out to a target or prospect.

This is something that I learned not in an investor meeting or client relationship, but *way* before I was a sales professional—and it stuck with me.

In my senior year at the University of Maryland, I waited tables at a pub on Thursday nights for extra spending money. Thursdays were our busiest night, so after closing everything down, I wouldn't get home most of the time until 4 a.m. or later. After just a few hours of sleep, my every-Friday-at-8 a.m. technical writing class would begin. It was one of those required must-pass classes to complete your major and graduate. If you worked a job in college, you feel the pain of this situation!

One morning, I accidentally slept through one too many of those 8 a.m. classes. Later that day, a message popped up in my .edu inbox from the technical writing professor. I called him Professor Grizzly, because he was grey-grizzly-bearded and cranky. His message said:

Ms. Gargan,

Your absence this morning was the third violation of my mandatory attendance policy. Unfortunately, as outlined in the syllabus, I will not be able to assign you a passing grade for this semester due to this infraction. You are welcome to re-enroll in this class in the fall, and no, I am not able to discuss this matter with you further.

I'll never forget that feeling of cold fear just washing over me. You know that feeling—where you are about to be *so screwed*?

If I didn't pass Professor Grizzly's course, I wouldn't graduate college. If I didn't graduate, I wouldn't be able to show up for my first job at the Baltimore City local TV station the Monday after I walked across the graduation stage. To say the stakes were high would be underselling this by about the size of the Terps football stadium.

Staring at the blinking cursor, not knowing what to write, I imagined that every blink was a light bulb flashing in my head: *think, think, think.* I started thinking about all the things I'd say to him to persuade him to show me some mercy. I was tired! I needed to graduate! I didn't have money for another semester! I had to start my new adult job in the glamorous world of television!

I realized after a few minutes that it was all about *me*. I, I, I. Grizzly had already warned me about my attendance, and he didn't care about my problems. I had to figure out what he *did* care about.

First thing Monday morning, I looked online, I went to the library, I went to the English department, I asked around, I read bulletin boards, I walked past his office. I was in total stalker spy mode. What did a cranky old professor like Grizzly care about?

As it turned out, I uncovered my opportunity online. On one of those early-2000s-era, proto-social-media message boards for the English department, I found out that Professor Grizzly was leading a department trip to Ireland in late summer. *Jackpot.*

I was a dual citizen with an Irish passport, and a former World Championship Irish step dancer—but more important than any of that, I had curated an awesome travel journal full of "locals only," off-the-beaten-path, non-touristy, legendary pubs in Ireland. Maybe he'd be interested in that.

It was the ultimate anti-touristy Ireland pub treasure map. But would it be enough to get me across the graduation stage?

I drafted and redrafted an email about ten times before I sent it, chewing my nails in anxiety.

Dear Professor,

In reviewing your attendance policy, it's clear that my absences are indeed wholly inexcusable.

On a personal note—planning a department trip to Ireland this summer? As a dual citizen and former Irish step dancer with family in the country, let me drop something off during your office hours tomorrow. It might greatly enhance your time there.

Grizzly wrote back one word. *Fine.*

The next day, I knocked on Grizzly's door. "Come *in!*" I heard, barked from the other side. I thought my heart was going to pound right out of my chest. Gathering what shreds of confidence I had left, I walked in as cool as I could and handed him the Irish Pub guide.

We began to talk about Ireland, history, travel—you name it—and thirty minutes later, it turned out that old Grizzly wasn't so bad after all. I almost forgot that this man held my professional future in the palm of his hand.

By the time I left, Grizzly told me that *if* I had a twenty-page paper on his desk by Friday, and *if* I didn't miss one single class for the remaining month of the semester, that he would *think* about giving me a teeny-tiny chance of passing his class.

Four weeks later, at the small graduation ceremony for the UMD English Department, I accepted my diploma. As I walked by a line of department professors, I locked eyes with Grizzly. He narrowed his eyes as if to say, "Those had better be some darn good pubs."

I showed up for my ultra-glamorous first job in television the following Monday morning. The lesson I learned from that experience was something I'd rely on for the rest of my career—I'd always remember that the pub map was the reason I'd walked the graduation stage. I had acted like a Friend. Most importantly, I had succeeded by being focused on the person I needed to persuade, not on myself and what I needed. This stayed with me to such an extent, and was so relevant through the next decade of my career, that I eventually named my persuasive messaging formula after that pub map: the PUB Method. I'll explain what that means in a few pages.

YOU ARE NOW RIDING SHOTGUN

How we do business has changed more in the last ten years than in the last one hundred. The way we consider solutions, learn about products and services, and are influenced to make decisions is irrevocably altered by our new social, mobile, and digital empowerment. Despite this, the majority of sales organizations struggle to evolve their processes and approach to meet the changing demands of the modern buyer.

As consumers, we are empowered for the first time in history to take charge of our own discovery and decision-making processes.

> Thanks to the internet, many buyers—particularly B2B buyers—are oftentimes fifty to seventy percent of the way through their buying process by the time they first encounter or engage with a sales professional.

Many of us in the sales profession still cling to an archaic notion of "let's educate this buyer from the top down, A to Z, so they can see how knowledgeable we are about our products and services." We think, *We'll seem like such smart experts and they'll be so impressed that they'll buy from us.*

Sometimes this is the case and it does work. But many

times, sales professionals will try to force prospects to sit through their "let's take it from the top" dog and pony show. From the buying side of the table, this is the worst.

I'm often impatiently thinking, *Dude, I wouldn't be talking to you if I didn't already know all this.* I want to talk price, implementation, logistics, and account service style—in other words, the elements that are difficult to learn and get a feel for just from reading the company's online marketing materials.

Evolving with the changing mindset of today's digital consumers is critical to our success.

According to Forrester Research, by 2020, one billion sales professionals will be obsolete.

When I first read that research, I rolled my eyes and thought it was a little far-fetched. Then something happened that made me realize maybe that wasn't such a ridiculous claim after all.

Do you remember buying your first car? I'll never forget when I did. It was right after my twenty-fourth birthday that I headed to a dealership in Towson, Maryland. I was determined to see if I could translate my newfound sales skills to get a good price inside the dealership. I read a ton of books on negotiation and car-buying tactics before showing up in my little suit and pumps ready to play hardball with the unsuspecting, super-nice sales guy named Tony. What I didn't read up on as much were the cars themselves. I figured I would shop around and make a decision when I got there.

When I left the dealership, I was the brand-new owner of the perfect car. It had been a *very* long process. Tony had spent *six hours* walking me through everything about every car to help me make a decision because, when I went in, I had no idea what kind of car I wanted—what color, what feature package, you name it. I was clueless! All I knew was the minivan wasn't going to cut it anymore. We went on test drives, I learned about engines, air conditioning, warranties, competitive models, leather, technology, and on, and on. Thank goodness I had Tony leading the way. The financing, purchase, and paperwork took another hour. It was such an intensive process, I almost fell asleep at the wheel driving the freaking thing home.

Fast-forward eleven years. Recently, my younger sister Shannon bought her first car, but her buying experience just a decade later was a tad different for several reasons, one being that she was smarter than me from the beginning of her process. To start, she researched every single make, model, option, and color available across the entire internet. She used an online car configurator to basically build her perfect car. She swapped out colors, packages, options. She shared it on social media and asked all her friends what they thought, and got their opinions and comments on what they were driving. She read all the ratings and reviews for the car she wanted, compared prices, talked to her bank. She lined up financing. She took her time and spent months ensuring the perfect purchase.

When she arrived at the same dealership I'd used, a few things had changed. Not only was Tony no longer there, but she didn't speak with a salesperson about anything other than paperwork and picking up her keys. Oh, and having the salesperson snap the requisite Instagram photo. Shannon drove away a happy new car owner. She was in and out in under an hour—and had no (real) need for Tony at all! So much had changed with the exact same business in just a few years.

That's when I realized: maybe that scary Forrester stat wasn't so outlandish after all. For most of history, when it came to the buyer's journey, sellers drove the car with the buyer riding shotgun.

These days, it's the buyer who's in the driver's seat.

SCREENS ARE THE NEW GATEKEEPERS

How many "get past the gatekeeper" techniques have you tested in your career? Or maybe you're new to sales and just starting to realize how important breaking through those barriers to get to the decision maker really is. Either way, today's gatekeeper isn't always a person. It isn't always a voicemail or a receptionist. Oftentimes, the modern gatekeeper is our very own laptop, tablet, or mobile screen.

Sometimes, not thinking through the reaction our messaging provokes on the other side of the screen keeps us from connecting with those who have the power to say yes.

We talked about how our inboxes are getting hammered with messaging every single day. You can probably attest to this reality in your own life, right? So, put yourself in your buyer's shoes for a moment. The sheer volume of inbound communication means, for the most part, that they don't have time or the interest to read your carefully-crafted narrative about how genius your company is. You have two and a half seconds—about ten words—to persuade them to even open your message at all. If those first ten words don't catch their attention, encouraging their brain to decide Friend or Server, they'll either scroll or swipe.

I recently came across an Entrepreneur.com post that

showed off a cold email template that the author claimed netted him meetings with twenty-two major executives. Since, at the time, I was researching for this book, I took the clickbait. Within moments, disappointment set in. The email was essentially a shorter, more polished version of "this is who I am, this is why I rock, this is who else thinks we rock, we can help you rock, can I meet with you."

The part that made me cringe was the first line—which he completely wasted—where he wrote: "Allow me to introduce myself; my name is XXX, President of XXX Company." He didn't disclose how many messages he had to send to get twenty-two meetings, but I'm willing to bet it was a lot. Hundreds.

I couldn't resist writing a comment: "I'm so excited that this worked for you, and I hear what you're saying on all these different pieces of this template. But unfortunately, unless my inbox is an outlier, the first line of your email is pretty identical to most emails I get from new vendors. When I see a mobile notification like this, my brain thinks Seller. I probably would not have opened this email, let alone read through all of these paragraphs. Even though it seems professional and well-written, I just wouldn't have gotten past your opening line."

I didn't want to hurt his feelings, since, as a fellow content writer, I know comments can sting, but I had to tell him the truth. You can rewrite your cold message template as many times as you want, but you're missing the most important part of attracting your recipient's attention: your opening line.

DROP THE NICETIES

⟨ Mailboxes   **All Inboxes**   Edit

Christine Masterson
Checking In
Hi Erin, How are you? How was your summer? Hope you enjoyed your time back East. I wanted to talk to you about...

If this came from someone you didn't know, would you read, scroll, or swipe? Your opening line determines whether your message gets opened. Your message being opened impacts whether you have a chance at opening an opportunity.

Within your first few words, your recipient's brain decides if a message is worth their time—and therefore, if *you* are worth their time.

Remember, the brain is judging you faster than it judges a Crocs-wearing Segway driver with a selfie stick.

In the first couple of words, who does your recipient's brain think you are? Can you avoid becoming scrolled or swiped? Can you avoid becoming part of the ninety-eight percent of ignored sales message carnage?

WHAT'S YOUR OPENER?

Take a moment to write down the opening line of your typical sales message.

If you could write that sentence down without knowing who your prospect is, there's your challenge right there. If you can recite your opening line from memory, it's definitely not personalized to your reader, and it will almost certainly make their brains categorize you as a suspicious Seller.

A lot of sales professionals try to bring conversational tactics that work in real life into the digital messaging world, but they don't translate well when delivered from behind the screen. For example, if you and I sat down to meet in real life, we'd exchange pleasantries and small talk, right? We wouldn't just sit down and dive right into business. We like to establish a shallow rapport about the weather, the office, the week, etc., before we dive into business. It's an expected social norm that, if skipped, would set a poor tone for the rest of our meeting.

According to the Harvard Business Review, a face-to-face request is thirty-four times more successful than an email.[8] Where the screen scrambles the etiquette of the real world lies here: If I get a digital message that says, "Hey Erin. How are you? Hope you're having a great week. We don't know each other, but..." guess what? You've lost me. A lot of times, I don't even get past "How are you?" because I'm thinking, *I don't know who this person is and I don't have time to find out.* That sender just maxed out their ten words with unhelpful banter. Worse, that unhelpful banter made my brain automatically choose Foe.

In a world where many of us yearn for Inbox Zero and message minimization, with every minute you spend crafting small talk for someone that you're trying to persuade, you're wasting their time and yours. Why? You're making them work even harder to figure out what you need from them—which they are probably too busy to do. On the rare chance that they do take enough time to confirm that you *do, in fact*, want something, they're even more annoyed. Now you've doubly pissed them off, and still wasted both of your time.

---

8   Vanessa K. Bohns, "A Face-to-Face Request is 34 Times More Successful..." *Harvard Business Review*, 2017.

THE SPREADSHEET THAT SAVED MY LIFE

In the years since I founded my agency, I've been on a quest to find the ultimate contractor/timekeeping/invoice management software. There are countless companies that provide various versions of this across multiple industries, with a dizzying array of features. Years ago, one of my employees made a thirty-tab spreadsheet trying to compare the features and benefits of each, from functionality, to pricing, to users, to how they bill, to reporting, to how intuitive their mobile app was to use. This software is one of the most important tools for an agency—and it's a *nightmare* to shop for. Especially since, as a creative, numbers and spreadsheets are my least favorite part of being a business owner.

I put a post on social media asking my network if they had any recommendations, which instantly made me software sales rep shark bait. My inbox was getting hammered even more than usual with a ton of different sales messages. I answered the first couple, not because they were great, but because the timing was right for me.

After responding to and meeting with the first ten people, my head was spinning. *This is mayhem. I cannot sit through one more PowerPoint presentation. My brain is going to explode. I can't tell one thing different from one brand to the next. They all seem the same, yet so different. So many spreadsheets. I need less numbers and copy, and more pictures and stories, please.*

One morning, just when I was about to give up and go back to our old vendor, I received the following message:

Vendor management software shopping? It can be really confusing with so many options. Here's a comparison chart with the most important features and pricing of the top five, plus us, of course.

Hope this helps,

Katie

Opening the chart, it was clean, basic, easy to understand, and laid out exactly what I had been trying to create for myself over those hours of being pitched to by countless fast-talking reps. *Yes!* Yes, yes, yes.

First, Katie had predicted and offered a solution to a major problem I was having, and she hadn't asked for *anything* in return! To say my attention was caught would be an understatement.

The second thing she did was provide truly useful content. That chart was a lifesaver. Not only was it super useful, it was, blessedly, *brief.* Instead of a long pitch or a PowerPoint, she simply reached out with a short, personal message and an awesome chart. I appreciated that, and the reciprocity reaction kicked in.

I bought from her, even though her company was more expensive, based in a different European time zone, and the product didn't have the same functionality as some of her competitors. I figured, if she was that intuitive in the pre-sale, she would take good care of me as the product evolved, and that's exactly what happened. Her company has been a great partner for three years. I even have her mobile number and can text her when I need something at an event or during a meeting, which is so appreciated in our world of limited-functionality chat and delayed back-and-forth messaging.

DIGITAL PICK-UP LINES

Let's be real. The parallels between online dating and online selling are endless—it's one stranger using the power of the internet to persuade the other to engage in a romantic or business relationship of some kind.

If you don't think digital pick-up lines are hilarious, you can skip this section. But if you love a little digital cheese like I do, read on. Before my husband and I got married,

I loved reading digital pick-up lines. I loved them on text, email, social media, online dating, everything.

Here are a few of the best ones I ever got from back in the day. How could you not laugh at these?

On a scale from 1 to America, how free are you tonight?

Was your mother a beaver? (Why?) Because DAMN-NNN, girl.

When you feel my sweater, you'll know what it's made of. (What?) Boyfriend material.

Is your name Google? (No, why?) Because you're the answer to everything I'm looking for.

I know I look tall in my pictures, but that's because I was sitting on my wallet.

If looks could kill, you'd be a weapon of mass destruction.

Why did I love these? Because they stood out from the majority of messages I received. They made me stop the scroll from ninety percent of online dating messages that said, "Hey"—yes, *hey*, or its horrendous cousin, "Wassup"—"You're Pretty," or, "Where are you from/what do you do/what are you into?" The last one was the worst, since all those questions were clearly answered on my profile.

I have several girlfriends still braving the online dating battlefield, and they share stories all the time about the men who persuade them to give them a chance. Typically, it's not rocket science. It's something that shows they spent time getting to know them before reaching out!

Iowa State? Go Cyclones! How did an Iowa gal find herself all the way West in Southern California?

Paddleboard company owner AND pharmaceutical executive? And I thought I was a hustler!

Poetry lover, eh? You might enjoy this YouTube channel of local poets doing the new "poetry improv" thing, it's pretty cool!

Some people go the exact opposite of the "Wassup" guy, and are a little *too* personalized, like the time my friend Kate received a completely personalized song, researched, written, and recorded just for her. The guy ended up being slightly too intense, as you may have guessed.

Digital persuasion essentially involves crafting the perfect opening pick-up line. It's a phrase that gets your recipient to lean in, pay attention, and ultimately, be moved to action. When online dating messages are appropriately personalized and stand out, the recipient is moved to act—numbers might be exchanged and exploratory coffee dates might transpire. It's the same with digital messaging. You want to open so personally, so targeted, that their brains register Friend or Server and they're persuaded to take action—clicking on your website, checking out your profile, or saying yes to a meeting.

At first, it might feel awkward to cold open and cut right to the chase, but in the modern marketplace, your window of opportunity for delivering the perfect digital pick-up line is only as big as a message notification or email preview.

Ninety-five percent of messages blow this window of opportunity, either on boring small talk or language full of *I, our, me,* and *we*.

Let's play out this scenario in real life:

> (You're sitting at a bar having a drink. A stranger approaches.)

> Stranger: Hi, I'm Joe. I'm a total catch who's gotten

great reviews from multiple previous dates. I have years of experience in dating, and I think I can meet your needs in the relationship marketplace. I wanted to find out if you'd be interested in setting up a time to talk about how we could potentially connect—

You: *Check please!*

Can you even imagine saying the above to someone? To their face? This sounds ridiculous, but it's a very real reflection of the messages in my inbox, and maybe your inbox. Don't be Joe!

Or, here's another scenario:

Stranger: Hi, I'm Joe.

You: Hi.

Stranger: It's nice to meet you.

You: You, too.

Stranger: I hope you're having a good day.

You: Um...

Stranger: I see that you're drinking a drink.

You: (*Eye roll!*)

Or this:

Stranger: How are you?

You: I'm good, thanks.

Stranger: I was just wondering if I can maybe have a moment of your time?

You: For what?

Stranger: I've just been watching you and I think I might have some solutions to that empty glass of yours. I'd love to take just a minute of your time to tell you about how I can potentially create value for you by refilling your glass.

You: Are you...trying to buy me a drink?

Stranger: I'm Joe. Here are some testimonials about previous drinks I've bought. Is there some potential here for a possible quick chat on the subject? Let me know.

You: Hard pass.

Stranger: Would it be all right if I potentially follow up in a few months to find out your evolving needs and how my solutions can meet them?

Can you imagine talking to Joe longer than the time it would take to pay your check and call a ride?

If someone's too aggressive, you don't want to engage. And if someone's too boring or too vague, same thing. How do you strike that sweet spot in between?

Try this:

Stranger: (Sees what you're drinking.) Old Fashioned, huh? You a bourbon fan?

You: Definitely. I'm from Kentucky, after all.

Stranger: Hey, go Wildcats!

This person has said exactly ten words to you, and not only are you engaged and wanting more, you're moved to action. You're probably exchanging numbers. This is exactly the type of action we all want to inspire in our recipients—but less than five percent of sales professionals are accomplishing this. The good news is that you have a huge opportunity to capitalize where they're failing.

MILLENNIALS ARE EXPERT IGNORERS

The more we get hammered with messaging from all sides, and the more social media consumes our lives, the better we become at ignoring and tuning out.

Older generations have a harder time doing this because they grew up with interruption-based messaging and cold calling. They're conditioned to answer their landline. They don't expect or depend on caller ID. If you try to sell to these people the old way, you'll probably have a small measure of success. They might be more open to Seller or even Foe messages, because they might have more time on their hands.

Millennials and younger generations, though, are absolute experts at ignoring. We (yes, I was born the very first year possible to be considered a millennial—I'm an old millennial) don't hear anything that we don't want to engage with.

If you think it's frustrating now trying to get people on the phone, get face time, or get them to answer your emails, just wait, my friends.

> The rising generation of bosses, budget holders, and decision-makers are digital natives. They've never known a world without the internet.

Even older millennials like me are pros at ignoring, and we're beginning to hold more positions of authority and power. If your sales techniques aren't working as well as they used to, the reality is, they're just going to continue to work less and less, until you're obsolete—like the sales professionals staffing the dealership the day my sister walked in to get a car she'd already mentally, digitally, and emotionally purchased.

You've probably felt this shift, right? It's going to get worse or better, depending on whether you choose to embrace the modern digital marketplace. The good news is this: making the shift yourself is *totally* doable.

If you want to stand out in a world that's changed more in the last ten years than the last hundred, you can, using my three-step PUB message formula. (More on what PUB stands for later.)

Maybe you're getting hung up on a lot. Maybe your calls are being ignored. (Do *you* answer numbers you don't know?) Maybe your emails are going unopened. Maybe you haven't booked a sales meeting in weeks, your manager is dropping hints about your quota, and you're just burned out by rejection. Or, maybe you're a successful entrepreneur just looking for new, creative ways to be even better at what you do. Maybe you're some combination of these. I've been in all three of those scenarios. I've been right alongside you: burned out, desperate, needing to pay the bills. I've been ignored and left wondering why what I was doing wasn't working. I've also been doing well but looking for ways to take success to the next level.

No matter whether you're a strong digital communicator or struggling to be heard online, this book will improve your digital persuasion power *fast*.

If you're motivated enough, and if you're brave enough, implementing the formula outlined in this book will drastically improve your sales success—one message at a time. Being digitally persuasive isn't what you learned in business school or in sales training. It's probably not what your manager tells you to do. It might not be in the pre-approved company metrics and sales strategy. But it'll blow your sales game out of the water. It'll completely change how you communicate and how people respond to you. Are you ready to evolve your sales strategy for the digital age?

WHY BUYERS IGNORE YOUR DIGITAL MESSAGES

What kind of sales training have you had? Maybe it was Dialing for Dollars and Coffee is for Closers. Maybe it was relationship selling. Maybe you've even sat through several "LinkedIn Light" programs, telling you to get a better profile picture and connect with everyone you meet.

For many of the world's biggest legacy companies, the aggressive-onslaught sales vibe still reigns king. For others, they are wading into the waters of "social selling" with uncertainty, trepidation, and annoyance. Most of them have duct taped together an attempted hybrid strategy of automating "personalization," while still advocating the quantity metric, which I have not personally seen working particularly well for any major organization in terms of growing sales. Frustration, yes. Sales, not so much.

The reason calls to action, aggressive asks, and stalkeresque follow-ups don't work is that, ultimately, people really don't like being told what to do. We've never liked it, but, particularly in this age of social and mobile and Google and Yelp and friends telling friends, you can't hammer people into doing things. It simply doesn't work in the new networked economy.

Have you ever gotten really pissed off at someone, then hammered out an email emptying your frustrations out onto that keyboard, saying all the things you wish you would or could say in person? Felt really good, didn't it? If you're smart, you just put that in your drafts folder and never sent it. Or, maybe you accidentally sent it and regretted it later. Either way, what is it about sitting behind that glowing wall of anonymity that empowers us to behave more boldly than we would in person?

There's actually a scientific reason. It's a psychological phenomenon called the *online disinhibition effect*.

The online disinhibition effect creates a disconnect between you and your typical polite, in-person interaction, because the wall of the computer screen offers you cover. Essentially, the anonymity of the internet makes you feel safe; you know that whatever reaction the person on the other end of the email has, positive or negative, you won't have to witness it. You won't have to see their face or read their body language as they respond to whatever you've written. You won't have to know if they're annoyed by your messages, because you'll likely never hear from them. The computer screen is like a safety blanket in this sense.

> **KNOWING THE SCREEN IS NOT INHERENTLY YOUR FRIEND IS THE FIRST STEP TOWARD IMPROVING HOW PERSUASIVE YOU ARE.**

Why *is* it so hard to translate who we are in real life into words on a computer screen? Why do we let the computer screen become a wall between us and the people we're trying to talk to? Why is there such a disconnect between our online presence and our offline, real-life personality?

You may also feel empowered by *asynchronous communication*, or communication that isn't happening in real time. That delay between sending an email and receiving a reply is like a safety buffer. It's different when you say something to someone's face: you can see their reaction, the subtle play of emotions across their face, right there in front of you. Through a computer screen, you know they're not even going to see your message for a while, and you probably won't hear back anytime soon.

The online disinhibition effect and asynchronous communication are two important aspects of the way we talk to each other today that are unaddressed in traditional sales strategies. Before we spent the majority of our days communicating behind screens, these nuances were unimportant to understand. But now, we spend ten hours a day behind screens, even though we're thirty-four times more persuasive face to face. Evolving your sales communication style to meet this reality is critical to success in the modern marketplace.

These psychological phenomena are what make cyber-bullying so prevalent these days. The computer screen empowers people in a negative way. Through a computer, when you're doing something you know is wrong, you don't feel like you'll get caught and you don't have to see your target in person, see their face fall, or feel their emotions. In sales, when we use the typical template, we pull a digital hit-and-run. We forget that our recipients are people, and we're essentially doing the same thing. I call it buyer-bullying.

It's kind of a gentler form of digital harassment, but it's still bullying! In terms of feeling harassed, at a certain point—after five unanswered messages and continuous follow-ups for months—it does start to feel a bit like harassment. It's an invasion of sorts, and the key takeaway is that the feelings of the recipient are *negative*. This type of online sales behavior registers as Foe to our recipients, loud and clear.

Here's a great example. I want to take you on a little journey I like to call "The Great Wall of Text."

Hi, Erin,

Thanks for connecting! Our company invented true mass one-to-one digital targeting for B2B and B2C by mapping over 180 million physical addresses to the IP address at that location. With this we're able to place digital display and video ads in front of people inside specific targeted homes/addresses with surgical accuracy while they browse the internet, without using cookies and with zero fraud or waste.

[TWO-PAGE WALL OF TEXT]

Let's talk!

Best,

John

My thought? *Thanks, John, for wasting my time, since I didn't ask and have no use for this. Foe!*

Two days pass.

Hi, Erin,

I'm following up on my last message because I think there might be a great partnership opportunity between our two companies, and I hoped to explore the idea with you.

[THE SAME TWO-PAGE WALL OF TEXT]

Best,

John

Repeat the above four times.

I found myself thinking, *Is this guy Foe real?*

At message #5, I sent the following reply:

John,

I'm writing a book on the art of digital persuasion right now. You're my primary example of what NOT to do. You have messaged me FIVE TIMES. WTF? Call me at 555-555-5555 so we can discuss improving your approach.

Thanks,

Erin

I didn't get a reply. I wasn't really expecting one, but it would have been nice. I really did want to get on the phone with this guy and gently explain how he was shooting himself in the foot with each and every digital message he sent. I wanted to help him understand that his recipients' brains were placing him in the Foe category, and that he was wasting his and his recipients' time.

BE BETTER THAN BULLIES AND BORES

Just like regular people who look extra cool on social media, or a coworker who seems rude on email but is great in real life, if you're an engaging sales professional, it can be challenging to translate that from behind the screen. In my experience working with hundreds of reps in multiple industries, most sales professionals message with two opposite approaches.

The first is trying to be tenacious, which comes across as buyer-bullying.

The second is trying to be professional, which comes across as buyer-boring.

Both are the opposite of digitally persuasive.

With a screen between you and your target, it's easy to see how one might become uninhibited to an aggressive degree—the buyer-bully, feeding on the lack of non-verbal feedback like body language and facial expressions. Similarly, without the non-verbal feedback, some sellers come across as over-professional, wasting time with boring small talk. Have you ever looked at an email you were writing and thought to yourself, *I need to edit this down!* Think about your reaction when you get a five-paragraph email from someone talking about themselves and what they need from you. You probably immediately mentally dismiss it, bored and annoyed.

As the sender, you've probably tried to find the right line to walk with your tone in order to get your message read. Have you ever felt like you've been sending messages into a void? With screens as the new gatekeepers, the wall between you and your recipients is taller and thicker than ever.

It's hard to find the right balance between aggression and politeness when you don't have non-verbal feedback to base adjustments on. Luckily, you're reading this book and what you'll learn will help you find that middle ground in between these extremes. Digital persuasion is the ladder you can use to climb over the wall of your laptop, tablet, or mobile screen.

Without the right balance, some sales professionals end up sending the most absurd messages of all time in a Hail Mary attempt to get attention. I'm sure you've seen some of these—I'm sure you've been on the receiving end of hundreds, actually, and your eyes probably roll as hard as mine. But the reason they get sent is simple: What's a potential buyer going to do? There's no door to slam in the sender's face, and you can't hang up on an email. Swiping delete just isn't as satisfying, but it's all we have.

If you want to be a Foe and a Seller—hey, do you. But it sounds like a horrible way to operate.

In fact, it *was* horrible. I know, because I used to do it.

I was a sales rep who called a hundred people a day—though I should say *bugged*. I *bugged* a hundred people a day. My sales conscience was giving me every physical sign that this was not okay, but my bosses assured me it was fine. I'd have that uncomfortable feeling in my heart, my pulse would race, I would sweat, I would squirm, I would feel guilty all the time. Who wants to feel guilty doing their job? The only other jobs where you feel guilty usually end in jail time, right?

I was keenly aware that relentlessly trying to sell to people in this way was wrong, but my bosses assured me over and over it wasn't:

They need what you offer.

You are helping them.

It's their job to learn about what can help their business.

Every "no" means you are one call closer to a "yes."

You never know until you ask.

Or, when I wasn't buying those lines, they would take a harder stance:

You are responsible for hitting this number.

You are responsible for getting them to "yes."

Toughen up or I'll find someone else who will.

This is your job. You don't have a choice.

How many times have you heard the same things from your boss?

As far as that last comment, in many ways my sales managers had been correct. Before social media and Google, we didn't have a choice. You had to knock on doors, call phone numbers, send emails, attend events, and touch as many people as possible because you had no other way of knowing who might or might not have a need for your widget! There was no other way to get to know these people without walking up to them, calling them, or messaging them and flat-out asking!

That's no longer true. It no longer has to be that way. You can access limitless information about people, companies, conversations, relationships, needs, news, products, competitors, commonalities, and care-abouts. Everything you could possibly need to know to sell smarter is right at your fingertips!

SELFLESS SELLING

When I moved around to the buyer side of the table, as a business owner, I realized how miserable I had been making people's lives, and I was ashamed that I had been that person. I was embarrassed that I had been an active contributor to ineffective, excessive, unwanted sales pitches via voicemail, email, and messaging.

What had I been thinking?

The challenge is that it's natural for most of us to approach messaging from our perspective. As sales professionals, for the most part we don't view ourselves as annoying; we ascribe go-getter vocabulary to what we're doing and view ourselves as *persistent, assertive,* and *confident.* Unfortunately, this mentality doesn't take our buyers' perspectives into consideration. That's a challenge my PUB message formula will help you overcome, one sentence at a time.

Thinking about your approach from the buyer's perspective does two things. One, it makes initial contact with your buyer more organic, which sets the stage for a better overall relationship. Two, it makes selling in today's age more effective, since you waste less time qualifying in person or reviewing solutions that are useless for that particular target.

ENOUGH ABOUT ME...WHAT DO YOU THINK ABOUT ME?

Nailing your perfect opening line is more important than keeping your head down for half a second longer than necessary after you drive a golf ball. You keep your eye on the ball, swing naturally, and then keep your eyes where the ball was, instead of immediately keeping track of it. That half second of visual control is the difference between whiffing it and crushing it.

But your opening line, like your opening drive, is just the

beginning. You can crush your drive with plenty of fairway left to botch the hole.

Your opening line might say "FREE BEER," but then if someone opens your email and you are slinging a new life insurance policy, it's the equivalent of an awesome drive followed by tree, bunker, overshot, undercut, triple-bogey disaster.

Here's a recent example from my own inbox:

Hi, Erin,

I just came across Socialite while working on a new sales and marketing system for a client.

It looks like you're offering social media marketing services for conferences, trade shows, and live events.

It seems your company shares a lot of similarities with a few of our clients. We work with businesses like yours who want to scale their business without worrying about all the marketing trends.

Recently, we showed a client how to generate $500,000 in new income in 11 days—and showed them how to build this into a scalable and repeatable process.

You open to having a quick chat?

Thanks,

Scott

See what this sales rep did? The first line mentions my business enough to let me know that he at least googled me. I did open his message. But then the very next paragraph launches straight back to being all about *him*. It's a bait and switch!

I care about you. (Open.) Just kidding, let's go back to *me*!

This is almost more annoying than the typical I, I, I message with no personalization. I felt like I'd been tricked.

Persuasion should always be used with a positive intention. It's for influencing people out of a desire to truly, authentically help them and form deep relationships. Whatever you're trying to sell or accomplish, it should be something you would feel comfortable persuading a friend or family member to do because you know it's going to help them in the end. Asking yourself whether you'd be comfortable doing that is a good indicator of whether you have the right intention. If the answer is no, it's time to rewrite.

Persuasion is very, very different from manipulation. Manipulation has a negative connotation, which is understandable; it means trying to *trick* people into doing things. Persuading someone to open your message is one thing. Manipulating someone with click bait, such as a false claim of a mutual friend, is quite another.

You should feel comfortable forwarding any message you write to someone you know. Ask yourself this: If you sent this to a friend of a friend, would you feel confident, or would you feel uncomfortable, shady, and embarrassed? The answer to this question is a great benchmark for identifying whether your message is persuasion or manipulation.

Here's another question to ask yourself: Would you pay ten dollars to send this message? Are you that confident that it holds enough value for you to invest in it reaching your recipient? If the answer is no, it's time to rethink your approach.

As someone who needs to drum up business, it's very easy to get caught up in the "eye on the prize/win at all costs" mentality. Maybe you have a quota you need to hit or you have payroll and overhead to meet—like I did. Maybe you have dreams of building a bigger business for yourself, or you want to get out of debt, or buy a plane. No matter what your motivation, challenge yourself not to be the person that's willing to try *anything* to get a response, even if it's essentially nagging your prospect (hint: it doesn't work for so-called "pick-up artists," and it won't work—in the long run—for you!).

Instead of focusing on yourself and your needs, can you see your buyers as people instead of prospects? Before you send a message, can you visualize what they might look like? Where they live? What they do? Before you hit send, can you honor your recipients with one moment of thoughtfulness to ensure your message will move them to action? Persuade them to engage in the beginning of a potential relationship with you? If you can, you'll get a lot further and much faster, because one thing is certain—no matter where you are or what industry you work in, pissing people off is the exact opposite of building likability and trust.

IGNORING IS EASY

So now we're in agreement that bugging a buyer is one of the fastest ways to be labeled a Foe or a Seller, which prompts a swipe to delete or a scroll to the wasteland. Ignoring or deleting both equal *no!*

Jeffrey Sussman
Grassroom x Socialite Agency
Hi Erin, I hope all is well. I just wanted to circle back on my
previous email re: Socialite Agency and Grassroom and a...

Jeffrey Sussman
Fit
Hi Erin, I have tried to get in touch with you to see if there is
a mutual fit between our companies and a way we could...

Jeffrey Sussman
Follow-up
Hi Erin, I wanted to check in and see if you had a chance to
check out Grassroom. As I previously mentioned in my past...

Jeffrey Sussman
Grassroom x Socialite Agency
Hi Erin, I'm following up to see if you had any time to check
out my previous email, or if you have another better way of...

Jeffrey Sussman
Call
Hi Erin, I hope you're having a great day. I was hoping to get
you on the phone sometime soon to discuss how our com...

Jeffrey Sussman
Intro
Hi Erin, my name is Jeffrey and I'm the Account Executive at
Grassroom. We work closely with brands like yours to change...

Updated Just Now
210,149 Unread

We've become conditioned to ignore this noise. It's kind
of like Times Square: all the flashing lights, noises, words,
images, and messages blend into one loud, colorful
experience. A tourist is going to stand there slack-jawed
and try to take it all in; a native who passes through the

intersection a hundred times a week is conditioned to tune it out.

Your inbox is exactly the same, I'll bet—and so is the inbox of every one of your buyers. When you get a daily truck-load of the same unappealing messages, they don't even register as separate emails anymore; they become one big block you can bulk-select and delete as one. Not only do most sales professionals get ignored, but they're probably not even a blip on the buyer's radar. Instead of improving their message to make it stand out, though, a lot of sales professionals will just keep following up, over and over.

Have you ever received messages that say, "I hate to bug you. I'm sorry to do this. I'm not sure if you got my last email," and wondered to yourself, *If you really hate to do this, then why are you doing it?*

These are the people whose sales conscience is tapping on their shoulder, like mine did. If that's happened to you, then it's a good thing you're reading this book, because it's time to evolve and improve your approach to new opportunity outreach.

DO YOU REALLY HAVE TO "BUG" PEOPLE?

From: relationships@growthcenter.c... ⌄

To: erin@eringargan.com >

hey
Today at 6:28 AM

Erin, I really hate to keep bugging you.

If we aren't a good fit for your company right now, that's totally cool, I just want to make sure we aren't missing out on an opportunity to help you if you need it.

Can you throw me a thumbs up or thumbs down? That way I'll know to focus my energy on some other projects.

Happy to chat with someone else if that's more appropriate?

Thanks!!

Kelly H.

Most sales reps use the same tactic with calls, but it's even less effective. To come back to a question I mentioned earlier: When is the last time you answered a number you didn't know?

Back in the days of Amos and the Baltimore City phone book, I called landlines. Most businesses didn't have caller ID, so you'd usually get a person on the phone. I'd make a hundred phone calls and get about ten appointments. Just ten years ago, that worked. Now, you have sales reps who leave voicemail after voicemail, because when people today see a number they don't know, they don't answer it, ever.

Cold calling is left over from the days before Caller ID and ubiquitous cell phones. Just typing out your cold call script, putting it in an email, and sending it off is a complete waste of your time. Digital messaging is a totally different medium, and traditional cold calling doesn't translate.

There's no point—you're not going to get a buyer on the phone just by calling them. They don't even have to check their voicemails. On most phones, they can read transcripts of the voicemail, see your outreach, and immediately delete it.

When you're actively using the PUB method outlined in this book, instead of letting the screen stop you, you'll be able to sell *around* it.

If you're not a natural writer or verbal communicator, perfect! By the time you're finished reading this book, that will no longer be the case. Despite the rise of video conferencing and messaging, written communication is the crux of digital messaging, and it's your best chance at reaching a new buyer.

Remember, standard email templates don't "work" (as I define "working"), because the majority of sales professionals are all using a similar one. I have hundreds of examples in my inbox; you could swap out my address and industry, swap in someone else's, and send them out in bulk. It's the exact same message. This isn't effective; it's just contributing to the cacophony of Foes and Sellers.

Noise gets ignored. How do you become the *signal* within that noise?

PERSONAL, USEFUL, AND BRIEF

Remember that time I almost didn't graduate college? I learned early on that effective and persuasive messaging is all about considering the personal perspective of your recipient. From the experience I had persuading Professor Grizzly to give me a second chance to the moment I deep-dived my own inbox and went through thousands of messages to find a pattern of successful persuasion, I taught myself the key to creating opportunities and building lasting relationships. This is the key I will be sharing with you over the next few pages.

In thirteen years of my own discovery and working with some of the world's biggest brands, I've developed a formula that leverages proven success patterns to craft a more persuasive way of communicating through the screen. I didn't have a good name for this formula until the day I remembered the first time I subconsciously used it—in the email I sent to Professor Grizzly offering him the Irish pub map. And it hit me: Be *personal*. Be *useful*. Be *brief*.

Effective digital messaging that rises above the noise follows these three rules:

1. Personal. Is this message leading with something highly personal to my recipient?
2. Useful. Am I offering something of actual value to my recipient?
3. Brief. Is this message shockingly short?

If you can craft your message maximizing those three steps, you will register as Friend or Server, and you'll avoid being categorized by your recipient's brain as a Foe or Seller.

You will inspire an action. You will ignite some kind of engagement. You will open an opportunity.

When you're not sure what to write or how to approach someone, just head to the PUB.

Sounds simple, right? Fair warning: writing a message that's Personal, Useful, and Brief can be challenging. In fact, it's usually much harder to be concise than to just write out a long sales pitch. Being succinct is always more challenging than showing up and throwing up. But taking the time to research and create the perfect PUB message is your digital differentiation edge. It determines whether you are heard or ignored. It decides whether your message is processed as Friend or Foe, Seller or Server.

Which one will your recipient decide you are?

TYPE LESS, SELL MORE

What you will love most about learning how to implement PUB into your digital communications is that while it requires you to mentally do more, you get to physically do less, all while financially and emotionally earning results that will change your life in every way possible.

We both know you're a rock star with sales in the real world, but you might be struggling with emails and social media because it's just not your jam. You may hate social media and email, but fewer people than you'd like are answering your phone calls, so they're a necessary evil. You have your existing relationships and referrals, but in trying to drum up new business, you might be struggling.

The good news for you is, according to what I've seen not only in my own inbox but also in working with global sales organizations, *so is almost everyone else.*

Here's more good news: there's a new window of opportunity open to you. You can get in there now and really stand out from the crowd before all the millennials and super-digitally-savvy Gen Z kids grow up and become the majority. You can get in on this if you just make a few quick tweaks to your approach and to how you think about persuasive online messaging to synch and match it with your persuasive offline abilities.

If you're copy-pasting and using a template a hundred times a day, obviously, you're not lazy; obviously, you're working hard. Who doesn't respect that work ethic? But with this formula, you will actually realize more results, while typing and reaching out less.

I respect hustle. But you can hustle smarter. With this book, you'll be crafting the perfect PUB message that will persuade your recipients that you are a Friend or Server worth meeting.

STEP 1: GET PERSONAL

Do you have anything monogrammed with your initials? Maybe you have a wallet or a ring that is personalized just for you? If you're from the South, like my husband, or the North East, like my sister-in-law, the answer is probably yes. The Eastern seaboard, from Boston to Alabama and beyond, is *obsessed* with monogramming. I once saw a guy in the Nashville airport with his head monogrammed. Calligraphy-style initials shaved right across the back of his head. Pretty intense. If you're from other parts of the country, you probably at least have a personalized t-shirt or something with your name on it.

We love feeling special. And there's something very special about an item that, in the entire world, can only belong to you (or someone with the same initials as you).

As a digital society, the internet has turned us into a personalization nation. From customizing our Starbucks on our mobile app, to Amazon recommending items just for us, to Netflix recommending shows for us, to flight alerts for places we want to go, to putting our name on literally anything via Etsy—the highly relevant, highly targeted, highly personal experience has recently become expected in all facets of our lives. Our Uber drivers even know our names and can play our personalized Spotify playlists while we ride. We don't eat, drink, buy, listen, watch, or read *anything* that is not highly personalized to us as individuals, so why would we engage with anything different when it comes to communications from people we don't know?

Remember when marketers first discovered how to automate emails with our names or company names in the subject lines and opening greeting? Remember when we used to believe it was actually a message that someone wrote us? Engagement rates on emails that use names and company names still far outperform those that don't; however, most consumers have wised up to the fact that J. Crew didn't send a message just to us.

The vast majority of digital messaging attempting to persuade someone new to give a stranger a chance starts with something like this:

Hi, Erin! Hope you are having a great day. I wanted to reach out because...

Hi, Erin, I see you are the Founder of Socialite Agency. I think you might be interested in...

On a mobile notification, the recipient will probably only see the stranger's name, and up to the word "I." This strategy is left over from the days when using someone's name made that someone think maybe this message was from a Friend. But our brains have wised up since then! Digital Darwinism has improved our brain's abilities to make faster and more accurate judgment calls on the true identity of senders. Our brains now know that a message like that probably falls into the Seller category. Depending on how busy we are at that exact moment, we may or may not open the message. If I don't recognize the sender's name, I typically don't.

While niceties of the offline world work really well to warm you up in person, online, it's the opposite. Polite small talk wastes a recipient's time. They're overloaded with messages as it is and just want to know who you are, what you want, and why you sent them yet another one when they ignored you already.

Persuasive digital communicators get right into what

they need. They don't waste their own time or their prospect's time.

Being personal doesn't mean just saying, "Hi, Name."

For example, a while back, my husband and I were spending some time in Charlotte, North Carolina. We like to live temporarily in new places just to check them out for short periods of time. We'd lived in Jackson Hole, Telluride, and Newport Beach, so we decided to try an upcoming Southeastern city where we happened to also have a large contingent of extended family. I have this weird challenge I always do when I go to a new place. I research notable people of the new location and then, using the PUB method, try to persuade one of them to meet with me for coffee. It works a lot of the time. Not all of the time. But the more I do it—the more it works!

When we got to Charlotte, I looked up the most notable people in town and found one of them is a guy named Jeffrey Gitomer. Here's a credential: he is the bestselling sales book author *of all time.* He's written thirteen *New York Times* Best Sellers.

You remember the "sales training" that I received the first day of my first job? *Go find people to buy advertising and we'll pay you a percentage.*

After the awesome first Amos the Amish deal (thanks to Kim), from there, I was on my own. Making calls, jumping in my car and driving all around Maryland with no idea what I was doing. My only guidance was Jeffrey Gitomer's *The Little Red Book of Selling* in my car. It was dog-eared and underlined and highlighted. I'd memorize some of the phrases in the book out in the parking lot, then literally walk in the door to try them out on potential buyers! A lot of times, they worked! That book was my only GPS in the wild world of local ad sales, and was my only real formal sales training when I started my career.

When I found out Gitomer lived in Charlotte, I was so excited. I spent days crafting a three-sentence message to him. It's so hard to be simple, but digitally persuasive people take the time that it requires. Remember, research is the new listening! I researched the heck out of him. These challenges are so fun because the more important your target is, the less time they have. Every word counts. There can't be any flaws, any excess. It's important to register as Friend or Server within ten words.

So, I wrote him a very short message.

It was Personal:

The Little Red Book of Selling author and his number

one fan both live in Charlotte? Your book saved my life back when I first started my career!

It was Useful:

Loved your podcast episode about the power of events in sales. Here's an article you might find helpful about the future intersection of sales and social at trade shows.

(Which is my expertise, but I didn't have to tell him that because, if the message persuaded him to check me out online, he would find that out on his own.)

It was Brief:

What is it like to be you?

Gitomer wrote back: Well, let's meet for coffee, and I'll tell you.

I was ecstatic. *Holy shit! I'm going to meet Jeffrey Gitomer. This is so rad.*

A few days later, I was sitting at a bagel place with him and his vivacious partner, Jen Gluckow.

"I can't believe I'm meeting with you," I said. "I'm so

excited. Can I ask—why did you even agree to meet with a perfect stranger?"

Jen told me in her New York accent, "Well, we saw your email, we googled you, and you looked like you had your shit together, so we decided to give you ten minutes."

We hit it off and shared ideas for the rest of the meeting. We ended up collaborating on a potential project and even doing a podcast together. Now that I'm back in California, I still follow their world-traveling adventures and super cute dog on Instagram, and would consider them friends.

Sure, it was nice of them to meet with me. Sure, it took a little luck. Sure, they happened to be in town; but, most importantly, I wrote a persuasive message and "looked like I had my shit together."

STEP ONE/SENTENCE ONE: WHAT TO WRITE

How do you lead with something personal to someone you don't even know, who doesn't know you? You use basic principles of persuasion to align your research and creativity to deliver the perfect digital pick-up line.

Dr. Robert Cialdini, another author whose work impacted my career, wrote a book back in the '80s called *Influ-*

ence: The Psychology of Persuasion. One of the scientific principles he talks about is the importance of "liking." Basically, if someone doesn't like you, you can't persuade them. Sounds pretty intuitive, huh? If it is, then why do some people still send messages saying, "Sorry to bug you again." Why would you like someone that is bugging you? Not persuasive.

Another one of Cialdini's principles is the principle of "social proof." It's a big part of why the Personal component of a PUB message is leading with someone or something that you both have in common.

Cialdini's research suggests that, in the modern world, we're all living in complex environments with a lot of stress. We don't have the time or energy to figure out what each person we come into contact with is really like, so we create stereotypes to help our brains process the information overload.

People tend to trust someone who was introduced to them by a mutual acquaintance. It's a shortcut. We want release from having to figure things out, so we rely on these shortcuts. If someone you know recommends another person to you, you don't have to analyze this new person and try to figure them out—you can just sit back and trust that your friend has your back and wouldn't introduce you to someone sketchy.

Hartman King thought we should connect!

Another way we think with stereotypes is to disregard all the relevant, available information and focus on a highly representative, single detail. This is why, if you don't have someone in common, something or somewhere in common works just as well. For example:

Skier, eh? Love Jackson Hole!

Maryland grad? Go Terps!

If you don't have someone or something in common, what about a mutual event?

AAPEX 2017 is almost here! Attending?

CES seemed crazier than usual this year!

What about an influencer or topic from a mutual event you both find interesting? This should be easy to find since you've researched your prospects to discover what they share, care about, and talk about online.

Simon Sinek's ISPA keynote rocked!

Cybersecurity threat panel posed some interesting questions.

Is anything happening in your recipient's world that is newsworthy?

Amazon acquisition? Congrats!

SVP promotion? Congrats!

Philips (competitor name here) new CT technology (product or service here) finally launched!

A pro tip to cutting copy is to lead right with the proper noun of personal significance and then put a question mark. While this would be an awkward way to communicate in real life, in the digital world, you can capture their attention with just one word of the notification, ensuring you won't be labeled as Foe or Seller prematurely.

Leading immediately with a proper noun that's personally significant to the buyer, ideally, a mutual contact or mutual topic of interest, activates "liking" or "social proof"—both extremely powerful persuasive elements of digital communication.

> ## CAN YOU CORRECT THE PAST?
>
> Go to your inbox and dig up the last cold sales message you sent. First, look at who you sent the message to. Is there anything in that recipient's world you could refer to in order to personalize the first line? Can you craft a perfect Personal opener and see how it changes your message? How does the inbox preview look?

NAMES MATTER

Have you ever had someone call you the wrong name? A big reason I don't advocate wasting space on using someone's name in digital communications is because, in this day and age, it reeks of automation, especially if someone you don't know is writing it.

I can't tell you how many times I've had sales reps, or people in general, email me and get my name wrong. They call me Eric or Aaron. Even if they get my name right, they get another detail wrong. A lot of people think I'm a guy because I have "CEO" as my title, which...don't get me started (that's a whole different book—I'll spare you here).

Everyone makes mistakes, but when it's consistently throughout the email: *Sir, It would be great if I could meet you, sir.* I know you didn't even take a second to look me up. There's no excuse not to look someone up before you reach out to them.

The more effort you put into thinking about your approach to each target, the greater the likelihood of someone actually reading your message, responding, and being persuaded. And you are wasting both your time and the potential buyer's time if you get their name, gender, or basic details wrong.

Another great thing about pledging to stop copy-pasting messages is that you never have to worry about accidentally sending the message to the wrong person with the wrong name!

CORRECT AND COMPELLING LANGUAGE

Have you ever gotten a beautiful message from someone, only to have it ruined by a glaring typo? Think about all your hard work researching and composing the perfect creative message, only to have it ruined by the unprofessionalism of a grammatical error.

Typos are hard to overlook, especially because there are endless apps and tools to prevent them. It's funny—people who struggle with spelling and grammar always say it like there's no helping it. "I'm just really bad with spelling."

The implication is, *deal with it, world.* But this is the digital age—there's an app for that! #DontBeLazy

Spell-check everything. Run everything you write through Grammarly. Typos make you look careless and incompetent. And once you look incompetent, it's basically *impossible* to build trust with a potential buyer.

To become a stronger writer, it's imperative to translate what's most powerful about your communication style into the digital space. One thing that can help with this is using voice-to-text applications. A lot of my sales reps who hate writing and aren't good at it find these apps really useful. They look at a picture of their prospect online, pretend that they're walking up to this person at a cocktail party, and just start talking. Their voice-to-text app records it.

The power of your words is also important; how can you make your two and a half seconds as compelling as possible? In the digital world, you don't have the power of your outfit, your energy, your hair, your smile, whatever your thing is with which you engage people. Words are your version of great hair, a great smile, and great energy.

Being thoughtful about your language choice means eliminating unnecessary or over-used words, like *I, the, good,* and *amazing*. Especially *amazing*. I'm on a mission to eradicate the word *amazing* from my vocabulary because *amazing* is the laziest adjective on the planet, and everyone uses it all the time! If everything is amazing, then nothing is amazing, and the word is meaningless.

Pamela Jett, a friend of mine who is an incredible speaker and author, preaches that hyperbole kills creativity—and I couldn't agree more.

WORDS TO AVOID

Words that hold you back from being your most persuasive self include *awesome*, *unbelievable*, *crushing*, *killing*, *totally*, and *nightmare*.

How often do you find yourself using hyperbole words? It's okay to use them here and there, as I have in this book, but beware of overdoing it.

I'm constantly searching for more powerful words. Thesaurus.com is a great resource to have open as you compose messaging. Words are your way to impress, so challenge yourself to make your vocabulary full of the best words. Download a dictionary app with words of the day.

It's enriching, and it will help you make your messages more persuasive.

Remember, to be persuasive, it's important to stand out from the crowd. If you're using the same language as everybody else, you're going to blend in.

Let's be real, though—don't take this to a ridiculous level and make every word a five-syllable SAT monster. Keep things simple, but also try to make your messages richer and more exciting.

CAN YOU DELETE YOURSELF?

iPhone, iPad, iMessage. We are living in a world obsessed with ourselves, and it's showing up in our language. Did you know that ninety-five percent of the messages I receive every day all start with the same word after the initial greeting? Can you guess which word?

Yes. The word "I."

By literally leading with themselves, the sender has completely wasted the opportunity to hook me in with something personal about myself, and instead has opened with a word that acts like I asked to know.

I just wanted to shoot you a quick email because I wanted to reach out and I would be more than happy to set aside some time to discuss how I could help with xyz...

I'm so sorry to bother you but I'm following up on my last response because I think there might be a great partnership opportunity between our two companies. I would love to tell you more about how I can...

I'd like to introduce myself. I am the SVP of Sales at XYZ and I think you might be interested in how I can help...

I, I, I. Me, me, me. These messages are all about the seller, not the buyer. Why would you waste your two and a half seconds talking about yourself, rather than about the person you're trying to reach?

If you look at executive messaging, they rarely use "I." If you look at intern messaging, they constantly use "I." It's the strongest digital communication indicator of how experienced you are in a matter of sentences. In fact, when I analyzed the one thousand sales messages from my inbox, something else I found was that non-management employees used the word "I" four times as much as management or the executive level. Using "I" is not only weak, ineffective, and self-centered, but it makes you appear extremely junior.

Intern:

> I think it would be best if I had all of us meet in the red room for today's meeting so I can use the Wi-Fi to research any topics of conversation during the meeting.

Executive:

> Let's meet in the red room for today's meeting so Wi-Fi will be available for any in-meeting conversation research.

Or, take a look at this before-and-after I did with a message I recently received:

BEFORE:

From: Jane Giovanni ›
To: erin@eringargan.com ›

How's RS going?
Today at 11:48 AM

Erin,

We haven't had the chance to connect so I just wanted to shoot you a quick email because I know sometimes researching new products can be overwhelming.

I would be more than happy to set aside some time to talk about what your e-signature needs might be.

AFTER:

E-Signature Solution Meeting
Today at 11:48 AM

Erin,

Researching a new product can be really overwhelming sometimes!

Perhaps you'd like to better understand how Socialite Agency can educate prospects with every outbound message?

Eradicate "I." *If you only take one thing away from this book, it's to erase the word "I" from your digital messaging.*

Hint: *this is harder than you think.* It's also possibly the most valuable tweak you can make to be more digitally persuasive.

The No "I" Challenge is a call for sales selflessness. It's really looking at what's going to help your buyer, because the power of digital persuasion lies in your intent to help someone get something they need or want.

ARE YOU UP FOR THE NO "I" CHALLENGE?

The next time you're typing an email, texting someone, or posting on social media—can you write your message without using "I"? You'll look more polished, articulate, and experienced—instantly.

Recently, I was on the phone with one of my clients helping her craft some messaging. She read me an e-blast she was going to send out.

I asked her, "Okay, how many I's do you count?"

She counted, then replied, "I count thirty-three."

"And how many you's?"

"Ten."

"Then we have a problem," I told her. We re-wrote the entire thing. Turns out we really only needed to use "I"

once, at the very end, when she said, "I hope this is helpful for you." When we were done, the entire tone of her
email had changed, and it was so Personal and Useful
that *I* was feeling persuaded by it. Be aware of your "I"
to "you" ratio.

The No "I" Challenge isn't just about removing a single
word for cosmetic reasons. It's a really a big deal.

Being persuasive is about standing out from the crowd.
How we do that is by shifting our focus one hundred percent to the other person. Selfless focus on your buyer will
differentiate you more than anything else. Eradicating "I"
is a physical way of stopping a message from being about
you and shifting it to being about your recipient.

I constantly go through emails and messages and ask
myself, *Is there another way to phrase this sentence?* If you
start to play around with it, you'll begin to notice that you
very rarely need the words "I" or "we." You can typically
remove them, especially when it comes to making things
shorter. Ninety-nine percent of the time, there's a better
way to say something, without using "I."

For example, a lot of times, you don't need phrases
like "I think," "I believe," "I know," "I feel." They're
implicit; obviously you think, believe, know, or feel these

things, because you're writing them. Saying the words is redundant.

Instead of writing, **I'm reaching out to you because I was talking with Hartman King. I thought it would be good for us to connect.**

Write, **Hartman King? Met with him last week.**

When you're looking at your messages, try to see them from a buyer's point of view. Would you answer a message like this? Would you open an email like this? Would you find this helpful?

Whenever I talk about the No "I" Challenge in a presentation or podcast, I get a ton of messages from people:

Oh my God, I use the word "I" constantly! I can't stop!

I was the same way, back when I was working on this problem in my own writing. At first, I used it all the time. When I challenged myself to get rid of it, I saw how unnecessary it was to insert myself and my POV into everything, when I could just cut right to talking about my audience.

Digital communication is at its most powerful when you

have a strong intent to truly help people, and when you're completely focused on *them*, not *you*.

Sounds like good advice for life in general, right?

The No "I" Challenge isn't just about becoming a better sales professional online. It's about becoming a better person and more impactful in *all* your relationships. You'll start to notice your communication improving throughout your life—with friends, family, spouses, strangers. It's a hugely positive change you can make in the way you interact.

JUST TRY IT:

1. Go to your sent folder in your email box, social media platform, or bulk mail manager.

2. Find an old message that either didn't get a reply, or didn't elicit the response you wanted.

3. Rewrite the message and remove the word "I."

4. Re-send the message. See the difference in the result of your message!

STEP 2: BE USEFUL

Getting Personal with your messaging takes research. Being Useful, though? That takes research *and* creativity.

So, how can you be more useful to your recipients? What can you "give" someone you don't know in just a few words?

In the days before the internet, sales reps tried to create a sense of reciprocity by giving you free stuff. They'd hand out mugs, pens, notepads, mousepads, shirts, bags—you name it. Random swag, basically. Who doesn't have a drawer full of the stuff? If you've spent any time in corporate, you definitely do.

I used to drop off gifts all the time. As a seller, I liked to go surprise clients with bagels for breakfast. Other sales professionals I know took their prospects to lunch, took them golfing, sent them bottles of wine...you name it.

There's still a deep-seated, psychological, persuasive principle in the offline world. Giving people things in the offline world is the way that you incite that feeling of reciprocity, of *I owe you.*

The other day, someone sent me a pen. And even though my logical brain was saying, *I don't even really write on paper anymore, what am I going to do with a pen?* the instinct part of my brain started to think, *I should respond back to their message, since they sent me a gift. I feel bad not responding, but I really don't want to change payroll companies.*

And I reminded myself that they were trying to activate this feeling in me, so don't fall for it! I didn't return the message because I really didn't want to change payroll companies. I liked the one we were using.

When charities send you free address labels, it's because they want you to feel like you owe them a donation. I mean, *they made you custom address labels.* Sure, it probably cost them all of twenty cents, but they took that kind of time. It's pure psychology, and it really works, which is why the nonprofit world has it dialed in. This is tapping into Personal and Useful (and Brief). So really, custom address labels are the perfect example of PUB persuasion executed perfectly!

In the social media world, "follow for follow" is a highly effective way to build your following. I follow you, you follow me. I like your post, you like mine. It's so powerful that there are companies that automate liking posts and following people just to activate the reciprocity back to their client's accounts.

Reciprocity is deeply ingrained in the fabric of our culture. Giving to receive is an ancient principle. But what can you give someone in a message? Ideas.

IDEAS ARE THE CURRENCY OF THE DIGITAL AGE.

In the social and digital space, reciprocity comes into play in sharing ideas on how to save time, how to save money, how to improve your skills, and productivity shortcuts. We lead such chaotic lives that anything that can help us relieve brain, wallet, or time strain is highly valued—a lot more than a free pen!

STEP TWO/SENTENCE TWO: WHAT TO WRITE

Figuring out what might be Useful to your recipient takes a little bit of creativity. Research your recipient's profile, posts, connections, and industry, and ask yourself the following questions:

1. Is there an introduction you can make?
2. Is there a recommendation for a place, restaurant, brand, or company you can offer?
3. Can you shed light on a possible threat to their business?
4. Is there any insider information you can provide that they might not have had?
5. Is there a helpful article you can send?
6. Is there a helpful app or gadget you can recommend?
7. Can you show them how something in their strategy or product might be incomplete?
8. Is there a creative idea you can give them?
9. Is there an idea that can help them save time, money, or stress?
10. Is there an event that might be exciting for them to attend?
11. Is there a person who might be helpful for them to know?
12. Is there a blog post that might help them solve a problem or ignite creativity?

And no, sending them unsolicited information about you,

your product, or your company is not Useful. Those types of communications are very useful, but only if they've asked for it. Not when you are trying to persuade a new person to give you a chance in a few short sentences. Sending "useful" information about yourself is a first-class ticket to Foe-ville or Seller City.

For example:

Hartman King thought we should connect! After speaking with him, it seems like you might enjoy this new venture capital podcast: *(link)*

Skier, eh? Love Jackson Hole! FYI, secret pre-sale of season passes opens for two weeks in August, you can save $1,000: *(link)*

Maryland grad? Go Terps! You might enjoy the SoCal alumni happy hour meetup next month in Irvine: *(link to event info)*

IBM marketer? Have you seen Forrester's new market research report they just published this week? *(link)*

AAPEX 2017 is almost here! Attending? Apparently, your ride from McCarran airport is free if you use Uber code *AAPEX17!*

CES seemed almost too crowded this year! Looks like some big brands are moving toward private events over show floor exhibits next year: *(article link)*

Simon Sinek's ISPA keynote—did you like it? If so (or if you missed it) you might enjoy his free eBook recapping his big points—it's exclusive to ISPA attendees: *(link)*

Cybersecurity threat panel posed some interesting questions. In case you missed it, here's a blog post recapping the key recommendations by General Hayden: *(link)*

Amazon acquisition? Congrats! You might be interested in this book about life after big acquisitions a friend sent me when we were acquired. It really helped with the transition: *(link to book)*

New SVP of Abbott Labs? Congrats! I've worked with Abbott in the past and know several of your new (potential) colleagues. Happy to share any of my insights/experiences with them if you think it might be helpful.

Philips (competitor name here) new CT technology (product or service here) finally launched! You might be interested in the product review Radiology Today published this morning: *(link)*

Remember, the goal of this message is not to sell them, so ditch your pitch. The goals of the second sentence of your message are to do the following:

1. Appropriately begin a relationship
2. Truly help a potential future friend
3. Ignite a feeling of reciprocity
4. Ensure that their brain categorized your message as Server, not Seller
5. Communicate for the click

If executed properly, you should receive a profile view, a website visit, clicks to links in your signature, maybe even a response or reply. You will absolutely have a new connection and will have opened up a new relationship. You have inspired them to see who you are and what you do, without shoving it down their throats. You have digitally persuaded them to be interested in you.

JOB CHANGES ARE PERFECT PERSUASION OPPORTUNITIES

If your target has just changed jobs, this is the ultimate moment where you can offer something truly useful.

When you reach out to them, the number one thing you want to do, as we've talked about, is make your message highly Personal and Useful.

Always start with people. Who do you know in common? Do you know anyone who works at that new company or has worked at that company? If you do know someone in common, try to think of ways that person might be useful to your potential buyer. Could they show your target the ropes?

Then think of other points of connection. Do you know clients they've had who can provide you with insight into this new company? Is the new company located somewhere you've lived, where you could offer tips about traffic or restaurants or schools?

Ask yourself tons of questions. *Where is this new job? What industry? Have I ever worked in that industry? Was there an incredible app or tool or website that helped me tremendously when I was working in that industry? Is there any information or an article or news about the company that I can share?*

Your target is in a change moment, and they have a lot of questions they really need answered. Look at their situation and ask yourself about everything you can possibly do to help them.

In doing this, you're coming from a place of service. That's your message when you reach out to them: you're helping them out. Lead with content that shows, *I want to help you in your transition.* By serving selflessly, you have just put yourself in the most powerfully persuasive position possible.

FROM HELPING TO HIRING

Sometimes, you may not need to rely on language alone.

Recently, I shared with my network that I was looking for some graphic design support for my agency. As usual, I got hammered with messages from a million agencies, vendors, contractors, and crowdsourcing platforms. I didn't know which one to choose. They shared their client lists, portfolio examples, pricing, awards, etc. All about them, of course, as usual.

One evening, a message from a designer named April stood out from the noise:

Wedding.com (one of our clients) has some great content on their Instagram. But it's a little copy heavy. What if instead of this (she used a screenshot of a post), you created a moving montage of images like this (and sent me a link to a private microsite where she

had created an example post for my client). Feel free to use this image for your client if you want!

The difference in the two posts was night and day. I didn't even know that you could create moving images in a static Instagram post—and it looked so dynamically different! The client was going to love it. Plus, April had just given me a free cool design that my team could upload right away, just in time for our weekly client review meeting. Wedding.com loved the new design idea, and I loved April for sending it! We hired her for a monthly retainer that was more than I had planned on spending; but, two years later, she is still worth every penny.

THE DIGITAL BREADCRUMB TRAIL

Depending on the industry you're in, you might have unlimited opportunities. For example, if you're selling skincare that actually delivers on the Fountain of Youth promise, and it's at all affordable, you're going to sell a lot of it to just about everyone. But if you're selling a high-ticket item, like a medical device or enterprise-level system that costs millions of dollars, you probably have a more limited prospect pool to message. Maybe fifty to one hundred potential buyers.

Every time you send a message that's ineffective, or even

downright offensive, you essentially shrink your prospect pool and you cut your legs out from under you. You blow that opportunity, because—and this is the most important thing to remember—you can't really reach out again. Technically you can, but most people would agree you are digging yourself a deeper digital hole. There are no do-overs. No message claw-backs.

In the digital world, everybody leaves a trail, and those breadcrumbs are forever. Have you ever heard the saying, "The internet is forever"? In the old days, if you reached out, made a crappy cold call pitch, and the buyer hung up on you, you might be able to wait six months and call them back with a better message. They wouldn't remember who you were, and you might be successful—maybe you didn't give your name the first time, or they didn't recognize you because they didn't see your face. Now, if you re-message someone on email or on LinkedIn or via text, there's a history of your messages. They'll remember, *Oh yeah, this is that a-hole who sent that shouty, pushy message, and oh, there it is, archived below the one I'm reading now.*

In digital, you don't get a second chance. That's what makes useless messages even more deadly. Don't waste your shot at becoming a Friend or a Server.

YOU'RE RIGHT, I AM SUPER BUSY

From: Tony Smith >

To: erin@eringargan.com >

interested

Today at 12:02 PM

Hi Erin - I know you're super busy but did you get a chance to look over the email that I sent you a couple of days ago?

I wanted to discuss about a potential partnership on a solution that can help increase sales for your ecommerce clients. However, I haven't heard back yet.

If you're interested in discussing details, please let me know.

ROI = RECIPROCITY OVERCOMES IGNORING

Going through those one thousand sales messages I'd received, I found that I responded to two percent of them. Of that two percent, I agreed to meet with sixty-five percent of the sales professionals who'd messaged me—so, more than half of them. And then I bought something from around half the people I met with.

Those are insane conversion numbers. Based on my small study, if you can get into that two percent, you have a really good shot at closing. That's around five times as much success as the other ninety-eight percent of sales professionals whose messages didn't get attention or a reply.

Yes, it's easier on the front-end to just blast, blast, blast,

blast; and from a numbers-game perspective, it *seems* logical. However, consider this: it's easier for you to send, but it's also easier for your recipients to ignore. Sending out PUB messages takes a little bit more work; but, on the back end, you will see your response rate and inbound actions increase tremendously.

DO YOU WANT TO WORK HARDER, OR SMARTER?

You can absolutely copy and paste one hundred messages for a one- to three-percent response rate, followed by a small close rate. Or, you can spend fifteen to thirty minutes per prospect, send a highly personalized message to five prospects, elicit a forty percent or more response rate, and close half of those. Doesn't it sound like a better use of your precious, limited time to work smarter, not harder?

It all comes back to serving, not selling. If you give, you will get. If you don't give, and you're just—as I call it—showing up and throwing up, you'll get ignored.

If you send a Useful message, you are going to get an answer simply because people can't help but send one. Ideally, though, you don't do it for the reciprocity. You do it because you want to help people. You want to be someone who's a connector and use those connections to improve your relationship currency, online persona, and opportunities.

People will always return the favor. They can't help it. Be of service—be *Useful*—and you'll see your opportunities flourish.

USEFUL MESSAGE TIPS:

1. Briefly picture the person you are sending the message to. Visualize what they look like, where they are, what they might be doing at that moment.

2. Think, *How can I serve this person?* Not, *How can I sell this person?*

3. Stop "letting people know" stuff. Phrases like, "I thought you might like to know"…"just to let you know"…"FYI"…"I thought you might be interested"…and "just to give you a heads up," are highly ineffective. They sound weak and generic. You want to sound cool and confident. Eradicate those meaningless filler phrases. In addition to the No "I" Challenge, try taking the No "FYI" Challenge.

4. Eliminate "I want." Lots of emails include phrases like, "I just want to connect," or "I just wanted to show you." The root of those sentences is "I want." Kicking off your message that way is the opposite of being your most digitally persuasive self. Do you think your buyer cares what *you* want? Ask yourself what *they* want. What is truly, specifically useful to *them*?

STEP 3: BRILLIANTLY BRIEF

Do you have a hard time being brief? Most of us sales professionals and entrepreneurs do. That's what makes us so successful in the real world! Our ability to capture our audience, tell great stories, and educate, entertain, and engage our prospects is oftentimes the key to our success. Unfortunately, those same powers of articulation don't do us any favors when translated for the small sales screen. I've received more three-, four-, and five-scroll emails from long-winded salespeople than I care to remember.

You've heard the phrase, "We always want what we can't have," right? One of Dr. Cialdini's principles of persuasion involves this idea of scarcity. It's why we want things that are the last one, limited time only, and exclusive. It's why we say we are giving up sweets or alcohol and, all of a sudden, it's all we can think about. It's why when you break up with someone you don't like, and then see them dating someone else, your mind immediately forgets the gross eating habits and cheap tendencies and lack of ambition, and thinks, "Wait, maybe I still like that person." It's why Vegas bouncers don't let people into empty nightclubs—to build the perception that it's hard to get in so people actually *want* in. It's why e-commerce sites tell you there's only a certain number of tickets, passes, or items remaining. When something is restricted, it's extremely attractive and our minds cannot help but want more.

I once rolled my eyes and laughed when my brother Brian, who is an excellent salesperson, told me he was in the business of "cultivating scarcity." Despite the buzzword overload, he was right, and it works.

There are several ways to trigger this persuasive feeling of wanting more of you and your messages by being shockingly short and blessedly brief in the last step of crafting your PUB message. Let's review a few of them.

INSPIRE TO ACTION

If your sales and marketing experience over the last decade-plus has been anything like mine, you probably learned that the most important part of your sales or marketing message is your "call to action."

As a result of that business commandment, a lot of pushy closing language is often included in digital sales messaging:

Let me know if I can help you.

Let me know if Tuesday works.

Let's talk soon to go over this.

Let me know if you have any questions.

When would be best for us to meet and discuss?

Don't miss your opportunity to get involved—reserve your spot now.

Does any of this sound familiar? Another question: Do you like being told what to do?

Probably not. Most people don't. Especially when you are

making an unsolicited ask of them. It's kind of the final nail in the coffin. Hi, me, me, me, more about me, and by the way, now I'm going tell you what I want you to do that works best for me.

Huh? Why would I do that? Why would I care what you want me to do? Why are you telling me what to do? I'm the decision maker. I am driving this car. And you, as a reward for your bossing me around, have now been downgraded from Seller to Foe.

Calling someone to action is pushy and aggressive. The reason brands and marketers do it is to create a sense of urgency, and when other brands weren't using that tactic, it worked very well. Conversion testing of CTA buttons on websites and ads is a downright science and can make a big difference in revenues. But when it comes to relationships, not revenue, it's highly inappropriate. In fact, calling someone to action actually has the *opposite* psychological effect. In testing hundreds of outbound digital messages, the more calls to action a sender makes to another individual, the less likely they are to take that action and the more likely they are to ignore or delete. Calls to action smell of advertising and most people hate advertising. Couple that with the fact that we are hammered all day with mini calls to action in the form of mobile notifications, and most people are really tired of their attention specks being demanded at all hours of the day.

There's a better way. Instead of calling your recipient to action, *inspire* them to action!

STEP THREE/SENTENCE THREE: WHAT TO WRITE

In crafting PUB messages, you're balancing science and art. The science is the psychology of your recipient, and it's where Personal and Useful help you out. The Brief aspect of the PUB message is all art. This is where you add just the right dash of your style. This is where you figure out how to really make the PUB message work for you, specifically in your own sales space. Experiment with scarcity, mystery, intrigue. Be different than every other desperate sales message begging for attention and action. Be above that noise. Be brief. There are two potential sign-offs to activate the perfect PUB response. Either no ask, or the clearest direct ask possible. These work because most people sign off with something in the middle—the vague request that creates too much work for your recipient.

The first is one I always recommend testing in the majority of my workshops.

It's the "Be Cool, Man" strategy. It's essentially confusing them, because most salespeople do not use this. It's different, it's interesting, it's organic, and it works. It's like the movie *Forgetting Sarah Marshall*, when Kunu says, "Do less." Sign off with something like this:

Cheers,

Happy Wednesday!

Hope this helps,

Good luck!

Congrats again,

Enjoy!

Have a great week,

Have a great rest of your day,

Let's stay in touch,

Nice "meeting" you,

A word of caution here is to beware of exclamation abuse, which can seem too eager. Only one exclamation point per message! And NEVER USE CAPS LOCK. It's the digital equivalent of shouting and the fastest way to get Foe-d.

The second sign off is the "Yes or No" sign off. These are for my workshop attendees who think approach number one is too airy-fairy, woo-woo, California magical thinking—and against everything they've ever learned—and that's fine. Again, this is the *art* part. This is where you test and learn and experiment with what works for you. There is no one-size-fits-all in PUB messaging! Different tactics work for different personality types and different scenarios.

If you're a direct person, and that works for you, then fine. Be that way on digital. Here's how you do it: instead of a call to action, ask your recipient a very specific ask. Make it crystal clear exactly what you want to them to do or decide.

Avoid generic, over-used phrases like these:

Explore partnerships
Mutual crossover
Pick your brain
Understand more about your business
Learn more about what you do
Get to know each other
See how we can help each other

These phrases put you dangerously close to Seller territory and can undo all the great work you did in your Personal open and your Useful offer. They are too vague, and they make your recipient have to do way too much work for the few seconds they're already investing in your message. Too much ambiguity around the ask elevates the risk level of failing to elicit an action. These phrases are perfectly fine later as the relationship progresses, but not in the initial first touch. The first touch is for igniting the possibility of a relationship. From there, you can start to engage with their posts, send them helpful things here and there, invite them to a cool event. From there, you date your prospect. They will look you up. They will know what you do. And if they are interested or know someone who might be, you will be the first to hear about it. Talk about true inbound relationship selling.

So, for the record, I am a staunch advocate that you ditch your pitch. But if you *absolutely* cannot do that and sleep at night, here are some examples of how you get straight to the ask without calling to action (as much as possible, being that you inherently *are* making an ask of them). Make it specific, relevant, yes or no, time and place, and very Brief. Do not sell in the message!

Hartman King thought we should connect! After speaking with him, it seems like you might enjoy

this new venture capital podcast: (link). Interested in meeting to learn about our portfolio on Tuesday at 10 a.m. (PST)? Let's Skype.

IBM marketer? Have you seen Forrester's new market research report they just published this week? (Link) Interested in seeing if our content marketing team can help you improve IBM's social media profiles? You'll receive a Zoom request for Wednesday at 10 a.m. (PST), if so.

AAPEX 2017 is almost here! Attending? Apparently, your ride from McCarran airport is free if you use Uber code *AAPEX17!* Interested in getting a coffee from 9–9:30 a.m. outside the conference hall on Tuesday to see if our accounting software can help your company save on your overhead costs?

CES seemed almost too crowded this year! Looks like some big brands are moving toward private events over show floor exhibits next year: (article link). Interested in meeting with me on Tuesday at 10 a.m. (PST) to see if we can help you organize a private event for next year's CES? You'll receive a request on Hangouts, if so.

Cybersecurity threat panel posed some interesting

questions. In case you missed it, here's a blog post recapping the key recommendations by General Hayden: (link). Interested in seeing a demo of our new cybersecurity hacker protection software?

Amazon acquisition? Congrats! You might be interested in this book about life after big acquisitions a friend sent me when we were acquired that really helped with the transition: (link to book). We help companies onboard new employees after acquisitions. Interested in meeting to see if we might be of service during this transition?

The key is to ensure that the recipient doesn't have to do any work or thinking, or make any effort beyond answering yes or no.

IMPROVING YOUR INTENTION

Remember, buyers' brains are reading their messages, trying to categorize you by asking, *What does this unknown person want?* Well, what you actually want is to sell them your product, service, or opportunity. But you don't say that, because then they're going to ignore you. Remember, they don't want to hear about *you*. You wouldn't say that at a networking event to someone you just met. You wouldn't ask someone to go out with you in the exact same few sentences as meeting them. It's awkward and inappropriate!

Try to shift your intention of what *else* you want: What you want is their *attention*, for them to be interested, for them to feel some kind of emotion. You want them to see you as a Friend or Server. Whether it's intrigue, whether it's worry, whether it's interest—you want them to feel something so strong that they cannot swipe you away or scroll past you.

Being Brief makes your recipient feel an emotion other than annoyance. It's not about showing up and throwing up. It's about being fascinating and attracting attention. Think of it like dating: the mysterious, quiet stranger nursing a drink at the bar is typically going to be more interesting and alluring than the person demanding all your attention and talking your ear off.

Oftentimes, the less said, the better. The smartest person in the room is usually the person who talks the least. They listen twice as much as they speak. It's brevity. It's scarcity.

People want more if they've only been given a taste; people want more of what has tempted them. And, if you've crafted the rest of your PUB message perfectly, they already like you, you have people or things in common, they feel like they owe you, and are now intrigued and wanting more. Why didn't this person ask me for anything? What's the catch?

They're going to check you out. Think of Brief as the reverse-psychology digital open. It's not a close, because you've persuaded them to open an opportunity for a relationship between the two of you. You closed them on the *potential* of a close. The step before the step. Progress!

THE NO-MESSAGE MESSAGE

In my training programs, the sales teams of large global organizations learn how to craft the perfect PUB message and how to infuse it with their own style that inspires the recipient to action. Consistent feedback is that there's one tip in particular that rises above the rest.

Most of the tips sales professionals learn are platform agnostic, meaning they work in email, text, LinkedIn, Facebook, wherever. The No-Message Message, though, is specific to LinkedIn.

Here's the idea: the best Brief message is sometimes no message at all.

What does that mean?

Have you ever been on LinkedIn and, in your notifications, you notice that someone has looked at your profile for the second time in a month? Disclaimer: you need an upgraded profile to access this feature, as does your recipient, so the efficacy of this is dependent upon those two factors.

You don't know this person, but they're clearly interested in you. You're probably compelled to at least click on their profile and check them out, if not click on their website and check out their business. Without sending you a message at all, they inspired you to action.

This is the basic structure of the No-Message Message:

1. On LinkedIn, visit the profile of the person you want to start a relationship with. If they have an upgraded account (many people do) they'll see that you looked at them.

2. Don't look more than once a week, and no more than three times total. I mean that: no more than three times! Looking too much is the digital equivalent of peeping through their bedroom window. "Creepy stalker" is not persuasive and is a close cousin of Foe.

3. They'll see you looking and be intrigued. They'll think and say, "Hmm, who's looking at me?" They'll click on your profile and check you out. That's an opportunity for a relationship.

The ultimate in Brief is no message at all, and it's the ultimate inbound lead.

Altruistic engagement is another awesome way to inspire action. This could be liking and commenting on someone's posts. Or, even better—depending on whether you're connected or not connected on LinkedIn in particular—identifying groups where your buyers or targets are having discussions, and going into those groups to comment in an insightful and respectful way. For example, I'm a professional speaker, and when I was initially drumming up speaking gigs, I joined a bunch of event planner groups on LinkedIn. I paid attention to what they were discussing and the questions they were asking. Since my agency specializes in social media for events, I'd seen and posted about plenty of cool, useful ideas that I was happy to share. One post in particular was asking for ideas on party themes, and a lot of lame or overdone ideas were being thrown out in response.

I popped into the thread and suggested a unique theme no one else had thought of (Overboard/Yacht Rock!), and offered examples of how we'd just run social media for an amazing event with that theme that the attendees had raved about afterward on social media. I didn't ask for anything in response or talk about my agency. I just took literally two minutes, dropped the useful suggestion, and moved on.

I got six responses from this one little forum comment. One of them turned into a $5,000 speaking gig right away. Another time, this same tactic pulled in a new six-figure account for Socialite. All of them earned clicks to my website, profile views, and, most importantly, new relationships built by being Useful.

Maybe people in your industry are not on LinkedIn, but this is the digital age—they're having conversations somewhere. Remember, *research is the new listening*. Find out where your targets are having conversations and go there. Join in. Be Useful. Offer ideas. Listen to their pain points. In doing so, you're introducing yourself *without* sending a standard sales junk message.

SHOCKINGLY SHORT SELLS

Brevity is *everything*. It's the make-or-break of being digitally persuasive.

Being digitally persuasive means using the power of language and positioning to incite action right away, right from the beginning. That's when you start to make the most of exciting opportunities because your target is paying attention. Can you use your powers of sales seduction in the first few words to hook the reader with something personal to them?

It's not just about a compelling opening—if the rest of your message is the dreaded Wall of Text, you'll get deleted. As we'll see, for a number of reasons, usually only the Brief messages get responses.

When someone opens your message, digital differentiation has already occurred if they see it's only two or three sentences. Visually, they see a short message, and they're leaning in because it's different, and it feels like something they can handle.

Today, TED Talks are viral, but that didn't happen right away. TED Talks had been on the internet for a long time before everyone knew what they were and started sharing them on Facebook. They just didn't take off at first because they took too long to get started.

The TED team would film starting with everyone walking into the auditorium and sitting down. They'd film the announcer coming up on stage and introducing the speaker. They'd film the full talk. They'd film Q&A. It was one long block of film, no cuts; each one was way too long and way too full of unnecessary communication.

When they analyzed their responses, they found that they weren't getting a ton of traction on these videos; people were clicking on them, watching the first couple seconds of the introductions, and clicking away. They realized that the introduction was totally meaningless to an online audience. If you're there in person, that introduction might mean a lot to you; on the internet, you already know who's speaking and what their topic is. It's in the title and description of the video.

The TED team switched up their filming to begin right at the end of the applause. If you notice, when you watch a TED Talk, it starts with the very tail-end of the applause after the introduction, and then it launches in right away with what's most important: the speaker's opening thoughts.

By changing just that one element of their production process, they hooked people in the first four seconds. Their videos started going viral.

You have just two and a half seconds to stand out. Put something specific about your recipient *up first*. You know when you get an email with a great subject line or message preview, and you click into it, only to be staring at a wall of text? You get right back out, right? Nobody has time for that. Everybody's trying their damnedest to move on from the shackles of messaging and live their real (or at least social media) lives.

Keep in mind that when you're having a hard time being Brief, it's useful to remember the *why*. Remember *why* you're writing the message. It's not to educate or sell them, or showcase your POV or mission statement; your goal is not to force them to listen to you. Your goal is not even to get them to agree to a meeting, unless that is the third sentence you feel makes sense for you. The goal is to *inspire them to action*. To communicate for a click. It's to move them to *do* something. Ninety-nine percent of the time, that action is not a purchase; it's a click to your profile or website, or a reply to your message. It's simply opening a relationship that could lead to a valuable opportunity.

WRITE NOTIFICATIONS, NOT DISSERTATIONS

We've discussed how small talk in your messages is a

waste of time for both the sender and the receiver. It's also a way for the important part of your message to literally go unseen. A lot of us check notifications on our mobile device. If you've opened your message with, *Hey, Erin. Hope you're having a great week. Blah, blah, blah,* you've sucked up precious real estate in the subject line, message preview, or notification, with words that don't matter and don't move anyone to action.

You have just a couple of words to stand out from the garbage and hook your target. It's imperative that you *get right to the point.*

Think about things in terms of previews—notification previews, subject line previews, LinkedIn previews. Those first couple of words should contain the crux of your message. That's usually all the time you get to convince someone to lean in before they scroll right past.

Another reason to be Brief is that most of us don't read as much anymore. Today, reading a book is such a luxury! You probably read on planes, because you don't have Wi-Fi, or on vacation. We *want* information. We crave it. We want to absorb everything that's happening. But we just don't have the same availability to sit down and take time to chip away at a wall of text. Make it easy for your target; make their decision to pay attention a no-brainer.

HOW NON-PERSUASIVE STACKS UP

Mailboxes **All Inboxes** Edit

Jane Giovanni
How's RS Going?
Erin, We haven't had the chance to connect so I just wanted to
shoot you a quick email because I know sometimes research...

Jeff Carter
Considering different career options?
Hi Erin, I was wondering if you might be interested in checking
out a new way to think about your career in the digital...

Groupon
Deals of the Moment
View All Deals

Tony Smith
interested
Hi Erin, I know you're super busy but did you have the chance
to look over the email that I sent you a couple days ago...

Hobie Surf Shop
60% off Everything Tomorrow at the Hobie Surf Shop
hobiesurfshop.com, 949.555.1282, San Juan Capistrano

Broadway Discounts
Open soon - you need to have a closer look
View an online version of this email. Save up to $40 use code
BDTC202 BUY NOW USE CODE

Updated Just Now
210,149 Unread

BEING BRIEF IS DIGITAL FRESH AIR

Think about when you get a message that cuts straight to
the point, doesn't waste your time, and gives you what

you need in a matter of seconds. It's so refreshing, isn't it? Before they've even read one word, just seeing the brevity of your message visually inspires an instant appreciation, an instant liking—you've been so Brief that they'll want to repeat the interaction in the future. It shows that you are not someone who is into time-wasting.

Say you're sitting down for a meeting at work. What's the absolute *best* thing you could possibly hear from the meeting organizer?

"All right, guys, let's keep this short."

Yes! It's a wonderful feeling.

The most valuable things in life are time and money. If you can save someone time, or save someone money, that kicks in the reciprocity principle; you've given them a gift. They'll respond by looking you up, replying to your message, referring you to someone else—the opportunities are endless, all because you kept it shockingly short.

UNCOVERING THE ASK

The other day, I got an email from someone who opened by introducing herself as working for a PR firm like this:

Hi, Erin, I hope you are having a great week. My name is X, I am the Co-Founder of X public relations agency.

My brain began registering her as a Seller, and so I deleted it because I thought that she was just going to say, "We're hoping that you would need PR services for your clients," or another similar sales pitch to hire them for PR.

The next week I got a second message from the same person. This time she changed her opening line to:

Socialite Agency would be a perfect expert guest for our weekly podcast.

If she had just led with a proper noun that got my attention (Socialite), and not "I am a PR executive and this is my company,"—if she had led with what she wanted, which was *me*—there wouldn't have been any risk. Because her message wasn't Personal or Brief, I almost missed the opportunity to be featured on her show.

Like many people, she had forgotten that if you send someone a message with something Personal, Useful, and Brief, they'll go check you out. They'll either google you, or they'll click on the profile in your email signature. You don't have to waste three paragraphs telling them everything they can easily find out on their own.

Being succinct is challenging. A simple message is much harder to articulate than a complicated one. Being long-winded and throwing everything at the wall is much easier.

As these examples have shown, though, the extra work to make your message concise is *so* worth it. When you send a brief, compelling message, your recipient will love you for it and will take action.

LEAVE VOICEMAILS IN THE '90S

Just this morning, I had three cold-call voicemails on my phone.

One was a software developer who wanted to build apps for Socialite. The message was a minute and sixteen seconds long. If that doesn't sound long, I invite you to open up your stopwatch app and watch seventy-six seconds tick by. It's an *eternity*.

If that sales professional had just written me a Brief, Useful message—something like, *Social media, huh? Have you checked out this app that helps agencies come up with meme ideas?* I would have thought it was rad. I would have clicked on his profile and I would have seen that he builds apps. Then I would have thought to myself, *Wow, that was really nice. That guy gave me that really cool app. What a nice dude.*

Respectful. Personal. Useful. Brief. Oh, he builds apps. Do we need any apps? Do we have any clients that need apps? I wonder, do I need an app guy? Maybe I should just meet with him to see what they do, in case we ever need an app guy.

That's the thought process of a buyer who's enticed. But his voicemail that went on, and on, *and on,* for more than a minute, left me bored and annoyed. *Delete.*

DIGITAL SALES REINVENTION

Maybe you've read all this and you want to create an even briefer message, but you're unsure how to edit down the message you typically send?

I'm going to recommend something radical: you should delete it.

Take your "features and benefits" spiel that you have memorized, and torch it. Torch it, because your features and benefits are not moving anyone to *feel* anything.

Your goal is to attract attention by making somebody feel something, and then incite an action. You are *digitally igniting* emotion.

If what you're doing now isn't working, isn't igniting anything—if it's fizzling out—are you brave enough to blow up your canned marketing pitch? Are you courageous enough to start over and do something different?

What if you radically shift the way you think about communication in the modern marketplace? What if you start over and write a PUB message that's totally new?

GET SHORTY

Try out being shockingly short with your next message.

First, go through the last ten unique sales messages in your Sent folder. Get a word count on each and find the average word count across your typical outbound message.

Then, cut that number in half. Yup, I said it—in half! Aim for two or three sentences *max*. Remember, the goal is to communicate for a click, and to inspire some kind of action, not to try to sell them within that one message. You want to sell them on giving you a chance, not sell them on your entire product, service, company, or idea.

Rewrite your message and restrict yourself to the above number. Make sure to send it out and track your response rate so you can compare it to the wordier messages you were sending before. Watch your response rates improve dramatically!

HOW TO IDENTIFY PERSUASION OPPORTUNITIES

For a digital communications expert, I have a very dirty secret: I love reading the newspaper. Like, the actual physical newspaper. It reminds me of sitting next to my dad growing up. It reminds me of taking the train into New York City for my internship one summer, with all the Wall Street people reading the newspaper before there was good Wi-Fi on trains. It just feels classic and nostalgic.

Every morning, I spend an hour reading the Wall Street Journal. By then, my tea has kicked in and I'll move back to digital, where I move right into the news that really matters: opportunity news. The best way to scour opportunity news? Sign up for email alerts from targeted social media groups.

Recently, I landed a new client who was a meeting planner. I spent some time going through meeting planner groups on sites like LinkedIn, looking for conversations. In one group chat, meeting planners were talking about the best way to get people to share what's happening at your event on social media. I weighed in, giving them the top three things you should look at doing.

From this one comment, I had twelve meeting planners view my profile. Three of them reached out, and we set up meetings.

It isn't always so easy; sometimes I have to keep looking around for weeks. But I know that's where to find those new opportunities. Part of being persuasive is being patient and consistent with your research. It's kind of like being a digital detective.

IS TIMING REALLY EVERYTHING?

In the offline world, sales professionals know to go to the right networking events and to be involved with advisory boards and volunteering. They know to talk to everyone at bars and restaurants, not to mention anyone sitting next to them on a plane. They know to always ask a million questions of everyone they meet, because you never know who knows who. But how can you use social media to find out if there's an opportunity to sell to someone?

Often, it's all about timing—like coming upon the perfect new discussion in a group chat, the way I did. There are other signs there's an opportunity to make a sale as well:

- ♀ Someone looks at your profile or accepts your invitation on a site like LinkedIn
- ♀ Someone gets promoted
- ♀ It's someone's birthday or work anniversary
- ♀ Someone is mentioned in the news
- ♀ Someone updates something in one of their profiles, like a summary or a photo
- ♀ Someone comments on, likes, or shares one of your blog posts
- ♀ Someone endorses people for skills

All of these moments are potentially a good time to reach out. But the biggest opportunity of all?

THE JACKPOT OF PERSUASION OPPORTUNITIES IS WHEN SOMEONE CHANGES JOBS.

If you've been at your current position for a while, this might sound familiar to you. The longer you stay at your job, the more complacent you get. You care less and less about changing the world and improving things. Whereas, when you leave a job, you're charged up with all the energy you let lie dormant while you were in the safety zone.

Someone switching to a new place of employment might need to move where they live, too; they might need a new computer or new clothes. They're in a transformational moment where they're primed to say yes. Monitoring your network for job changes is essential and can provide a huge loophole in an otherwise complicated corporate knot.

It can take a long time—and sometimes a lot of observation—but by mining through people's content, you can start to see what their deepest concerns are and what really matters to them.

You can cast a huge net and just blast a billion people with a generic, cold message, or you can whittle it down to your fifty most targeted prospects. When I work with my sales teams, they know exactly who their targets are. They know where they work. They know what they care about. They absorb all the information easily found with some research around the web. Stalkerish? Not if it's publicly available information. And it might be a tad social stalker, but it's also tremendously *effective*.

Don't be afraid to get appropriately stalkerish. Otherwise, you're going to miss out on valuable insights you can use to convert leads into opportunities.

Social media is out there and, yes, *everyone* is on it, but ninety-eight percent of your peers and your competitors are doing a horrible job of leveraging it. Most people trying to sell me something haven't even made an attempt at due diligence. They've done no research before reaching out. These sales professionals aren't looking for the opportunities; they're not *listening* to digital conversations. They're not connecting the dots to find people in common on the personal side.

KNOW YOUR TIMING TO SAVE TIME

Timing is one of those things that has to be seen to be understood, so I'm going to launch right in here with some examples of classically bad timing:

1. About a year ago, I had just hired a new video team to help with some international events. My LinkedIn post said, "We're so happy to be partnering with this video company on project X!" Later that afternoon, a competitor video team reached out and asked if we wanted help with video support. With a canned, templated sales message. *Did you even look me up at all?* I thought. If they had, they would have seen that *just that morning* I had posted about our partnership with an identical video vendor!

2. You sell a nice-to-have service, not a need-to-have service, like an employee wellness program with massages (although you might argue that massages *are* a need-to-have!). You reach out to a company that just lost a huge client, and probably won't be taking on additional expenses anytime soon. The client loss was big enough that it was in the news. You'd have found it if you'd done any research before you reached out! Better timing would be after the company gains a new huge client, which you'll also see in the news if you do your research.

3. You sell relocation services, and you reach out to a company that just changed headquarters. Why are you reaching out if they *just* relocated? Obviously, they don't need you—the opportunity to persuade happened months ago, before they made the move.

Timing is everything. It's the difference between striking the iron while it's hot and being left out in the cold. It's the different between looking competent and looking foolish. Good timing is built through careful research and monitoring. Do you know your prospects well enough to predict their next move, and thereby plan yours? Save your time by knowing your timing.

PERSUASIVE "WHY CHANGE?" MESSAGING

One of the techniques you may have learned as a sales professional is "Why change?" messaging. These are messages aimed at buyers you're looking to turn from your competitor's product to your product. In other words, it's a message that says, "Here's what we have that our competitors don't have, and why you should buy from us."

Most of the messages I get are "Why change?" messages. I can understand why people send them, but they're not as persuasive as they used to be. They seem left over from the Coke or Pepsi, AT&T or Verizon days. Bud Light or Coors Light?

No matter how convincing you are about what you're selling, people make decisions more often based on risk aversion. You're more likely to be persuaded to do something based on someone explaining how that will protect you from losing something. That's why the more effective approach is saying something like, "You could lose all your data unless you upgrade." Or, one of the fastest-growing industries is identify theft: "You could have your whole life stolen, but if you spend $90, you're protected."

This is caveman psychology. It takes us back to our basic instincts and fears of losing the things we need for survival. *Hold onto what you have* is a lot more powerful than the idea of what *could* be. If Choice A is to go hunt someplace unknown for a chance at something awesome like better food, and Choice B is a device that will hold onto the food you already have so you'll never lose it, most people will choose Choice B all day.

Another challenge of the "Why change?" technique is that when people don't stand by their decisions or don't do what they say they're going to do, they're labeled undesirable. They're flakes, dodgy, sketchy. They made a bad choice the first time around; what makes us trust their new choice this time? I've worked with so many teams who have their same vendors for years—and they know they are doing a terrible job—but they hired them, so admitting the vendors were the wrong choice also means admitting *they* made the wrong choice. Especially for larger corporations, where the game is job defense, not job offense. In some of our country's largest enterprises, it's always better to avoid a mistake then to take a risk, even if that risk could potentially create a win.

Recall the big change opportunity: switching jobs. Your timing is perfect to approach someone within the first ninety days of their new job or role within the organization. Their goal is to find new solutions and vendors, and to make decisions to get points on the board that the person before them couldn't. They're more open than usual to accepting new ideas or changing course on systems and routines. They're almost expected to make big decisions in the first few weeks to show that they are already "helping" their organization. After that ninety-day window, however, that person is more likely to stand by the decisions they've made to avoid seeming scattered or flaky. They are also more worn out from meeting with new people and vendors and just want to make a decision—a decision they will probably stick with for the duration of that role.

This is essentially the root of why people hate change: it says to the world, "I either made a mistake on my first choice, or I'm being flaky—I'm all over the place."

There are only a few situations where sending a "Why change?" message really could work. One is when there's a trigger, an opportunity—something job-related or event-related. This is why constantly researching and monitoring the social web for potential moments like these is crucial.

The best "Why change?" situation is if someone the buyer trusts introduces you. This triggers instincts of association and affiliation. Basically, the buyer thinks, *If my friend trusts this person, then I trust them, too.* This transferred trust is the most powerful opportunity timing of all.

MOMENT MONITORING

If you've read this far, you know that looking for opportunities involves in-depth research—stalker-level research. There are paid tools like Sales Navigator and free tools like Google Alerts. There are more high-level monitoring tools that come out, fold up, and evolve all the time, so just have a Google session and see what's the latest in this space to keep tabs on the events that most greatly impact your prospects.

Know your people. Know who you're trying to persuade, and research before you reach out. Google them, look at anything they've posted. Read the articles they comment on and do your homework.

Again, this sounds basic, but for whatever reason, *most sales professionals aren't doing this.* The path is wide open for you to make the biggest impression in the buyer pool; with just a little effort spent on each prospect, you can cruise right past your competitors with a major first-mover advantage.

HOTTEST DIGITAL PERSUASION OPPORTUNITIES

1. An introduction by someone the potential buyer trusts

2. A change in the potential buyer's life, especially a new job

3. Big changes in the potential buyer's world (global events, industry-wide changes, etc.)

4. Directly (within twenty-four hours) meeting in person at an event or meeting

OPTIMIZING SOCIAL SELLING SUCCESS

You now have the core formula that will evolve your digital sales messaging to be more persuasive to prospects in the modern marketplace.

You've learned how to write the perfect PUB message, why it's important, and how you can use digital persuasion to sell around the screen and create new relationships and opportunities.

Now let's kick it up a notch. You've seen the basics; here's how to optimize my strategy to yield the best results and create exactly the sales life you want and deserve.

CONSTANT CONNECTING

The most digitally persuasive professionals gain access to as many people as possible to get as much information as possible.

One way to do this is to constantly think about making connections. For example, even if you are scheduled to meet with a prospect in person, ideally, you've already connected with them on social media before the meeting. Or, if you meet someone at an event, can you connect with them right on the spot from your phone, ensuring you have their contact information? Sometimes social media search functionality is not the greatest, so it's good to type in their name and show them the list and say, "Is that you?" Or, if they aren't popping up, you can type your name into their phone or app, or call or connect with yourself from their phone to ensure the connection was secured.

Whoever you're dealing with, or hoping to deal with, vaguely reaching out with, "Let's connect," isn't optimally persuasive. Try not to send a request with an auto-generated message. Use the PUB method right away, rather than connecting with them first and then sending the PUB after.

HELLO, STRANGER!

Have you ever had that experience of meeting a stranger—at a bar, a restaurant, an airport lounge, a party, anywhere—who ultimately turned into a valuable contact? Connect with anyone new you meet in person, however briefly, on social media. You never know if they might look you up and have an opportunity—or vice versa! You never know who knows who or who does what—but social media does!

Constant connecting isn't just about connecting the offline and the online; it's also about growing your online connections. Mine your online networks. Constantly look to see who knows who and who can make important introductions. Conversely, clean up your newsfeeds by unfollowing irrelevant people, companies, and media outlets. Whenever you open your mobile social media apps, you should see relevant people and information within the first two to three scrolls. If you don't, it's time to do some connection cleaning.

SHOW, DON'T TELL

In a super-saturated digital environment, images are crucial in helping you stand out. Ninety percent of the information sent to the brain is visual, ninety-three percent of all human communication is visual, and our brains process images 60,000 times faster than words. We can understand an entire complex concept with one image. Or, even better, an image can explain something that maybe words can't express, or that's too difficult to convey in words.

Let's say you share a mutual connection with your target. You send a photo of you with that mutual acquaintance and write, *Meghan and I had so much fun at the gala last week! Heard all about your company!* and that's it. Your target will most likely be intrigued and write back something like, *What? How do you two know each other?* Now the ball's in your court to capitalize on that opportunity.

Whether it's sports, family, geography, industry, hobbies, or even something simple like a big movie that just came out, there's so much potential for common ground with your target and so many great ways to discern where that common ground is for the two of you.

It's important to remember that images aren't a replacement for words, but rather an enhancement. Either you write two or three great sentences, or you write one or two great sentences and add something visual, like a .gif, a meme, or a YouTube link. Your strategically persuasive sentences are still essential.

Here's an example of someone using an image to really enhance their message. I was in Hawaii for a marketing conference a few years ago, and some National Volleyball Tournament was also happening at the same time. A paid search management firm rep wanted to meet with me and get coffee. He sent a link to the YouTube video of Tom Cruise and Val Kilmer playing shirtless volleyball in *Top Gun*. He wrote:

Not to enter the danger zone, but if you're not too busy watching studs play volleyball, do you want to get a cup of coffee and talk about XYZ at the event?

I laughed out loud. Partially because it caught me by surprise, and partially because I had planned on sneaking over to catch some of the action. *Sold.* I agreed to meet him for coffee before the next day's session, and we had a great conversation.

Whereas, if he had messaged me with something like, **Hello, Erin. My company is blah, blah, blah, blah, blah. We're going to be at the same marketing event and should explore mutual crossover in the search space,** I probably would have ignored it.

When it comes to digital communication, think big and creative. Think differently, write differently, communicate differently, because most messages really suck! Most people are using the same uninspired approaches, and even the smallest bit of effort and creativity means you will stand out dramatically from your buyer's pack of inbox wolves.

Put bluntly? Be interesting!

DON'T BE JOE. JOE IS BORING.

From: Joe Allen
To: erin@eringargan.com

Re Web Solution & App Development
Today at 7:36 AM

Hi Erin,

My name is Joe and I represent an enterprise Mobility and Web development company.

We can provide you following services at affordable rates-

Mobile App Development (iPhone/iPad, Android)
Web Application Development (PHP, .NET, Python)
Enterprise Application Development (Web, mobile and MS technologies)
CRM and Field Force Management
ERPs and document management system
Employee Management System

I would like to know more about your business requirements and can also be available for a phone/Skype call for project discussion.

HOW BUYABLE ARE YOU?

To echo my friend Jen Gluckow from earlier in the book, "Do you look like you have your shit together?"

If your message persuades me to actually stop what I'm doing and check you out, what would I find? Someone who looks credible, knowledgeable, trustworthy, and likeable? Or someone who conveys a different impression?

If a potential new relationship is going to check you out online, which is arguably the most important purpose of the PUB message, it's critical that you make sure your personal brand is ready. You may already know some of the common mistakes people make with their professional profiles. Even if you've avoided these mistakes, there are several proactive things you can do to make your online presence more polished.

For one, don't show off. If you're shouting about yourself and how successful you are when you're looking for a job, a recruiter or a headhunter might think, *Oh cool, they're the man/gal/person.* But think about your profiles from the buyer's perspective. If they see that someone has earned President's Club ten times in a row, or that they're a "top producer," what do they think? *Ooh. A really good salesperson. Probably going to pull a bait and switch. Slick-talking*

salespeople make me nervous. I don't want to get talked into
anything I'm not ready for. Better stay away from this one.

Being a really good sales professional doesn't have the best connotation from a buyer's perspective. There's a stereotype of slick wordplay, clever tactics, and the advantage being weighted in favor of the seller, not the buyer. Knowing this, how can you build trust as soon as you can?

Think about the kind of buyer you're hoping will look you up. Identify language that's familiar to them. Use this buyer-centric language and update your profile language, presentations, and visuals with your buyer in mind. Set yourself up as a thought leader, with a bio catered toward how you help clients who are just like the buyers looking at your profile. Showcase why your buyers should want to connect and engage with you. Amplify testimonials from other clients who are similar to them.

We've talked about the importance of liking. One of the things that make us like people is attractiveness. There's a reason why more attractive people are in positions of power, why sales professionals are good looking, or why they send good looking people to hand out samples. Being attractive is an element of the liking principle, which is what persuades people to ultimately decide to make certain decisions.

It's surprising how many people have poor quality or inappropriate profile photos online—or, even worse, no photo at all? I've seen arms cut out, pets, partners, kids, sunsets, mountains—these are all not helpful to a buyer who wants to size you up. Studies have shown that many people subconsciously decide within two or three seconds if they like someone based on their social media profile picture. What does your photo convey?

There are a lot of different rules about what makes you likeable in your profile photo. For example, you don't want to be smiling too big with tons of teeth showing, because you'll look cheesy and untrustworthy. Buyers will wonder, *Why is this person so happy?* You don't want to be scowling, like you're getting a mugshot, either. Then buyers will think, *Uh, this person is probably hard to get along with.* You want to be somewhere in the middle.

Invest in a professional photo, and make sure that your photo has been taken in the last five years. Nothing is worse than engaging with one person online but then meeting another in the real world—it erodes trust just when you've started to build it.

MODERN MARKETPLACE MONITORING

Getting to a point where inbound digital persuasion is a possibility starts with making yourself visible.

We touched on this briefly in the last chapter, but let's dig a little deeper here. Are you constantly monitoring what's happening around your target, their competitors, companies, product names, industry names, and industry publications? You want to have alerts set up so when something hits social media or hits the press or hits the internet, it's coming right to your inbox and you're able to respond and react to it. You can use Sales Navigator, Google Alerts, or another one of the dozens of platforms out there. It's very easy to set up, but a lot of people don't take the time to do it.

When I look through those thousand messages in my inbox, it's evident that most people either don't take the time to research, or they research so superficially that it's very obvious they're just trying to build a false rapport. *Hey, Erin! I see you work in social media. Me too! We should connect.* Awesome, dude, but that doesn't automatically make us friends!

Successful digital persuaders constantly scan for openings and opportunities. They're always looking for moments when they could be of service. These include events like mergers and acquisitions, job changes, product launches, executive firings or hirings, relocations, industry news, regulation changes—even larger political changes. An election can be an opportunity if you know what you're looking for.

Digital persuaders are voracious digital listeners, because it's difficult to be persuasive if you aren't listening to what the person is doing, saying, and needing. This way, you can be creative enough to craft that perfect one- or two-liner that is Personal and Useful.

MULTI-THREAD CONNECTING

Another key component of being persuasive is having the power of the majority on your side. It's not about just finding that one person, that single-thread relationship.

Do you know who your buyers' influencers are? Can you develop relationships above, below, and beside them? Who do they report to, who reports to them, and who's on their level? You can uncover these answers by figuring out who they are, connecting with them online, and making sure that you're showing them love and attention on social media. If they post an article, build on the relationship by liking it. Just being on their radar is fuel for the relationship.

Socially surrounding your target ensures two things:

- ♡ You are well known by everyone on the team. Most of the time, with big decisions, there's more than one buyer.
- ♡ You're protected. If your target leaves, you retain that contract and then you also get the next contract.

YOU DON'T GET A SECOND SEARCH TO MAKE A FIRST IMPRESSION

When you send the right PUB message, an interested buyer should be able to find all the information they could ever want or need: pitch decks, videos, product information, and press, all on your profile or on your website, or wherever you exist online.

This information, as well as your overall online presence, is what will persuade someone to take the next steps and move your budding relationship from online to offline. Moving the conversation off of digital and into the real world is mastering the art of digital persuasion.

Your online brand is the first impression most buyers will experience. When you google yourself, are you comfortable with that first impression? If you aren't sure, ask a trusted client or friend to look you up and see if the person you are in the real world is positively and accurately portrayed in the digital one. If the answer is no, it might be time to do a little online brand optimization.

Here are a few classic things to avoid:

COCKTAIL PARTY ETIQUETTE TOTALLY TRANSLATES

Sometimes, I get messages from people who actually do a pretty good job with PUB. They hook me in a little bit, so I go and check them out. And what do I find?

Politics and religion. On *LinkedIn*.

Are you kidding? Inappropriate! And you just alienated who knows how much of your audience! I click away.

Keep the politics and religion confined to your (private, ideally) Facebook or Twitter. As strongly as you hold your beliefs, not everyone shares them, and you run the risk of alienating potential buyers if you make them your entire persona.

TYPOS ARE PSYCHO

Sometimes, a sales professional actually nails the PUB message, and they sound pretty smart, so I go check them out. Then their profile has a billion typos and grammatical errors, or sloppy mistakes and missed words.

If they can't pay attention to their own online profile, what on earth would make me think they're going to pay attention to me, their customer?

Spell-check! Grammarly! Or, even better, make friends with a writer or editor and ask them for a thorough copyedit of your online profile in exchange for some great wine. That bottle of Cabernet will pay huge dividends in the future.

DON'T GET GHOSTED

Someone approaches you online, and their message is compelling. But when you go to their profile, they don't have a picture.

Sketchy.

You google them, and they're a ghost. They have zero footprint. They literally don't exist on the internet. Not on social media, not anywhere.

Really sketchy.

Look, I'm not suggesting that everyone has to be super

active on social media. But if you're reading this book, you're someone who's trying to find success in an industry where, if you don't exist on the internet, *you don't exist.* It's important to have some kind of online presence. If you don't, your competitor does. Period.

PHOTO FAUX PAS

The number one online profile mistake? Terrible, unprofessional, *horrendous* photos. This is another point we've touched on briefly, but let me emphasize this again. Over the years, I've identified the worst repeat offenders, and I'm sure you've seen them, too:

- ♀ A group shot from a wedding where both of their arms are cut off because they think they look good, so they cropped out their buddies.
- ♀ The dreaded sunset photo. Hint: if you're backlit, we can't see your face. I'm looking at a faceless blob in front of a sunset. *Next.*
- ♀ A photo of them on a hilltop or something, taken from far away. Great, I can tell that you have a basic human form, but if I ever ran into you in an elevator, I would have no clue it was you!

Right, wrong, or indifferent, we are a culture that judges by appearances. We judge people in the first couple seconds we see them. Having a flattering professional photo is taking a big step toward the best A-game that you can possibly bring.

A professional photographer's work may not be that much better than today's iPhones, but it sends a subliminal message that says, *I'm very invested in my professional brand, to the point where I made a major effort to put my best foot forward.*

The subtler nonverbal message is, *How I represent myself is important to me and, if I rep you, your account will also be important to me. I'll put the same effort into you as I did into myself.*

It's the classic sales strategy of always presenting yourself as polished as you possibly can. Hair, nails, outfit, everything. If you don't bring your best physical self to the table, you risk this thought from a potential new buying relationship:

Well, if she can't take care of herself, how will she take care of me and my account?

Avoiding these mistakes will make you look competent and professional. You never know which one of your messages is going to resonate and entice someone to check you out.

You don't know how many people are going to google you or look at your profile. What if, in the split second they see your profile pic pop up, they decide you don't seem professional, likable, credible, and trustworthy, so they just click away? You just lost that opportunity, and you can never get it back.

TAKING A LOOK IN THE MIRROR

After reading through those thousand sales emails and seeing the patterns in the way most sales professionals communicate, I've come up with three persona categories that many sales professionals unfortunately fall into.

THE DIGITAL NARCISSIST

Me, me, me. I, I, I.

Hi, Erin, I wanted to discuss a potential partnership on a solution that could help increase sales for your ecommerce clients. However, I haven't heard back from you. I'd love to connect—please let me know.

Yup, because it's all about you, dude!

Hi, Erin, thanks so much for the connection. I am a former Wall Street executive and World Record holder...

Bragosaurus. Delete.

Hello, Erin. I wanted to reach out and let you know about a new product we are debuting...

Whoops, I fell asleep.

You get the picture. Stop talking about yourself! I guarantee your target doesn't care about you *half* as much as they care about themselves.

THE DIGITAL STALKER

This is someone who will message you (or, more likely, set up automated messages) a million times in a row without any hint of interest from you in return. This is the opposite of digital persuasiveness—this is digital harassment! There was this one guy who "followed up" with me *five times*, with the same old message, slightly tweaked, over and over. I got so pissed off I started harassing him back, so he'd know what it felt like (is there such a thing as inbox rage?). He finally answered me, and I demanded he get on the phone with me.

On the call, he admitted to me that his messages were actually coming from someone he hired in the Philippines to hammer out cold messages all day long to everyone across the entire web. He was getting about a 0.02 percent return. So, every week, after pissing off five thousand people, he'd have, at most, ten new appointments.

Case closed. Don't automate. Don't hammer. *Personalize.*

THE DIGITAL RANDO

A majority of the messages that I get—that all buyers get— don't answer the most crucial questions of all: *What do you want? Why are you messaging me?*

These sales professionals don't want to seem salesy or pushy, so they go the other direction, with aimless messages that go on forever: *I'm glad we connected, I love connecting with smart people, I hope my network is valuable to you, I wonder if we have mutual crossover. Who knows? Guess we'll find out someday.* Or the worst one is, *Tell me what your company does,* or, *Tell me about your clients.* Why should I do your research for you?

Get to the point. Have a reason to message your targets, and state that reason explicitly. Don't beat around the bush. Everyone's too busy to guess why you're talking to them—just say what you mean! For example, take a look at how long this person talks around his message before asking me for a meeting:

GET TO THE POINT!

From: Jesse Sansen ›
To: erin@eringargan.com ›

quick question
Today at 8:05 AM

Hi Erin,

I understand that you're the Founder and CEO at Socialite
Agency and the best person to speak with.

We would potentially be interested in a strategic partnership with
your company. I'm referring to a solution that can help increase
sales for your ecommerce clients, by eliminating any common
issues like unsupported currencies, clunky security drills, bank
rejection or even unsupported card and payment brands.

Erin, do you have 5 minutes for a quick call, to show you how
exactly this would benefit your company?

Let me know,

Jesse

PROFILE POLISH

Here are some things you can include in your profile or
on your website to improve your online presence:

RECOMMENDATIONS

This is huge. This is social signaling, likability, affinity,
and word of mouth, all wrapped up in one. Get people in
your network to write recommendations for the work you
can do and the value you can bring. Your trustworthiness

will shoot through the roof and only increase with each new recommendation. Write a recommendation before you request one, obviously—reciprocity rules!

TESTIMONIALS

A lot of people have testimonials on their profiles, but they make the mistake of getting them all from people in one small facet of their professional life. It's more effective to have testimonials from all the way around you, about everything you've accomplished. Include testimonials from people that you managed, people that managed you, and clients that have hired you. Give your potential buyers a well-rounded perspective of what you can offer them.

TITLES, AWARDS, DEGREES, AND CERTIFICATIONS

Dr. Cialdini's *authority principle* includes the idea that when you have something that's conferred upon you by some kind of a credible institution or higher source, like a title or degree, then people view you as being more credible, trustworthy, and likable. You're providing proof that someone else officially validated your likability and value.

As a society, we're taught that if you have authority, you can be trusted. If you have a title, a degree, or an award, you automatically have authority. The work is done for your potential buyers—they don't have to take the time to vet you themselves; somebody else already did that. It's a time-saver.

Most importantly, you look *credible*. People don't have to figure you out for themselves.

At the end of the day, people choose the safest option—the one they know they can trust. Trappings and titles are proof of trust. Collect them, and they'll choose you more often than not.

DEMONSTRATING EXPERTISE

If I had to choose the most important thing you can do for your personal brand—besides taking a better professional headshot—it's thought leadership.

Contribute your thoughts to public forums as much as possible. Get your ideas out there. Then, if someone looks you up, they can get a feel for your perspective, what you sound like, and what your personality is like.

The other day, I published a post on LinkedIn. I immediately got five emails from old clients I hadn't talked to in forever. *I forgot how much I love your writing. When I was reading it, I could hear your voice. How are you? What are you up to? What is going on? Love this new website. Loved your point about social sales strategy.*

It reconnected me with valuable contacts I hadn't spoken to in years and reignited opportunities that had been lying dormant.

Creating content is a really powerful way to communicate your expertise, stay relevant, stay on people's minds, and share ideas—which, as you know, is the most valuable currency on the internet. Well, besides Bitcoin. People want to be inspired, and appreciate it when you share a new idea that will hopefully make their work or their life just a little bit easier.

CAN YOU WEIGH IN WITH A SENTENCE?

If you don't feel comfortable (or don't feel like) creating thought leadership with an original piece of content, like a blog post or a video, or even a short post, that's okay. Can you weigh in on existing conversations somewhere on social? Can you give your two cents in the comments at the end of a blog post, or in a group chat, or forum? It's not as visible, but *any* visibility is much more effective than social silence. You never know who is reading what post, who could come across your opinion or idea, agree with you, and want to hear more from you!

A LESSON FROM MAD MEN

Years back, I was asked to be part of a larger partner agency's team to pitch event management for the largest national sporting event in the United States. My team and I would white-label under this partner to run the social media component of the event. The opportunity was beyond mammoth. It's an event televised all over the world, with every celebrity you can imagine, tickets costing thousands a pop to attend—this opportunity was, literally, the big leagues. All the branding, the logos, the landing pages, the advertising, the TV commercials, the social media. It was a multi-million-dollar contract, and we had a shot to pitch for it.

I flew up to San Francisco, so we could all practice each planned portion of our pitch for two full days before the meeting. The plan was to walk through our case studies, our client testimonials, and how genius and creative we were, beating our chests. That's how marketing agencies rolled back in the *Mad Men*-era before the internet; there was no way to google anyone, so all the client had to go on were agencies walking in and confidently proclaiming to be the best. The only problem was that now, the internet existed. Yet this legacy agency was sticking to their same old presentation formula.

The whole thing felt very uncomfortable to me. I kept

thinking, *They can see all of our cases, our work, our reviews and recommendations on our website. Why are we going in here and just telling them, in a louder, more animated way, everything they already know? If they didn't, they wouldn't be agreeing to meet with us.*

But emotions were running high. This was a table of ten senior creative marketing executives, each one of us was an alpha with a big personality and bigger ideas on the right direction for the pitch. We were low on sleep and lower on caffeine. As the youngest on team by about a decade, I was lucky to have been included in this pitch, and knew I should keep my mouth shut. To my horror, in our internal prep meeting before the meeting with the client, I found myself suggesting out loud to a team of edgy, tired, seasoned ad veterans:

"What if we ditched the big intro about us and just opened with something that went wrong for them last year. Then we could come up with three creative ideas about how we would have taken a different approach to solving or even avoiding it in the first place?"

Personal, Useful.

I also tried to think *Brief.* We had two hours for our presentation, but that seemed excessive.

"Also, these rehearsals are leaving us only twenty minutes for Q&A, and that's if we don't each go over our time. What if we just prepare a half-hour presentation, cut the rest, and have an organic conversation for the rest of the time, where the client can drive."

The faces around the table glared at me in a mix of annoyance, anger, and impatience. To say the team was less than impressed with me and my ideas would be putting it lightly. There were a few seconds of stony silence.

"So just wing it?" one creative director asked. "Are you insane? That's suicide."

Knowing I was low on the totem pole, and just a contractor, I backed down.

The day of the meeting, we went into a huge, shiny room at the client's headquarters, filled with top-level executives. The conference table was miles long and the coffee they brought tasted incredible. It was the biggest pitch I've ever been a part of in my entire life.

We were forty-five minutes in when the decision maker, who was at the very head of the table, said, "Um, guys, this is great, but we know all this. We know you guys rock.

We saw you. We googled you. We want to hear ideas about how you can help us."

Our preparation about ourselves far outweighed our preparation about the client and the whole meeting began to slowly sink, like the part in *Titanic* where the ship breaks in half. Everyone on our team started talking at once, over each other, fighting for the spotlight, making up crappy ideas on the fly. It was *terrible*. The client ended the meeting early, and basically politely threw us out.

This was, by far, *the* most blown opportunity I've ever seen in my entire life. This was the client that got away. My little social scope of the contract would have easily been our biggest project to date. It would have been huge. And this was a sports client, for a sport I was obsessed with, so it also would have been *so much fun*, a dream come true.

We totally botched it. It was painful. It was awful. I wanted to die. You know those comedies where the whole foundation of the humor is secondhand embarrassment? Cringeworthy humor, like *The Office*? That's what this was.

It was a huge mistake, and I learned some major lessons from it. We weren't Personal, Useful, or Brief. We were talking about ourselves. We were trying to sell the way you used to sell before the internet existed. Think of that—

we pitched like we forgot the internet existed. How terrible is that?

Since then, in every client presentation, I've never led with anything about us unless the client asks or invites me to. I lead with what problems we can solve and ideas for being helpful that are specifically personalized to that client. Watching the event a year later on television, the rejection still stung. That was a lesson I never forgot.

UNDERSTANDING THE CONTRAST EFFECT

Have you ever wondered why we are so obsessed with our competitors? It has to do with what is called the contrast effect. The contrast effect says that when you experience two similar things in succession, your perception of the second is heavily influenced by the first. So, the more messages and options that cross your buyer's brain, the more competitive your playing landscape becomes.

Imagine you're shopping and you see a great pair of shoes. You think, *YES! These shoes are perfect.* Then another pair of shoes is brought to you and you think, *Ooh, I might like these even better.* The more options, the more complicated the game.

The rapid, relatively recent rise of mobile, social, and

digital networks has greatly contributed to the explosion of the idea-sharing economy. You may have been able to be persuasive in your own way in the old days. Today, in comparison with all the other options your buyer has access to, you might be unknowingly losing out in areas you didn't even realize.

As in most things in life, the 80/20 rule applies: eighty percent of great content and thought leadership is being created by twenty percent of the people online. So, it's not unrealistic to assume that twenty percent of those content creators are probably persuading buyers to give them a large percent—maybe even eighty percent—of the best business.

The evolution of the modern marketplace means digital business has become a lot more competitive than it used to be. The twenty percent of leaders who are creating eighty percent of the content are *really* bringing it. They're publishing LinkedIn long-form posts, they're broadcasting on Facebook Live, they're constantly writing and sharing ideas, and they're developing all kinds of creative ways to educate and engage their potential buyers.

Here's the one thing you know for sure: your buyer has a need, and they're going online to find someone who can help them solve that need. Why shouldn't it be you?

All you have to do is lean in as much as your competitors are, or, better yet, set the leader pace yourself. Buyers are Googling, they're scouring Yelp and Facebook, they're searching for blog posts and articles about their interests and challenges. *Be a voice in that crowd.* Can you have some kind of presence, even if it's a small one?

IF THEY LIKE YOU, THEY WILL COME

Throughout this book, we've talked a lot about the concept of likeability. Another reason liking is so important, and another reason it's important to examine how you present yourself online, is because we instinctively *agree* with people we *like*.

It's almost impossible to be on the same page with someone you don't like. If the most brilliant ideas in the world are delivered by someone you don't like, you won't be able to get your head around complying with them. This happened to me just the other day. I was in a client meeting with a bunch of really nice people, and this one super sour woman kept arguing with everyone. She was abrasive and rubbed me the wrong way. Yet the more I listened to her, the more I realized she was actually absolutely right. I kept trying to tell myself she wasn't just because I didn't particularly care for her energy.

Don't annoy people online and destroy any hope of like-ability! Your ideas might not get the audience they deserve because they weren't delivered in the most persuasive way.

If you reach out to somebody and make a great first impression, and you share something helpful and have a great conversation, that person will like you. And if they like you, it's way more likely that they're going to agree with you and buy what you have to offer.

So, liking is really, really important. When you create your online profile, your online persona, are you likable? Do you seem like a nice person? It sounds so simple as to almost be trite, but it's crucial. *Do you seem cool?*

Digital persuasion is all about research. It's all about digging. It's about figuring out what your target likes and what they're into. What do they read? What articles do they share on social media? What do they comment on? Where do they live? Do they have interesting hobbies that they've written down in their profile? Are they sharing photos of themselves volunteering or skiing on Instagram?

Once you figure out what your target likes, you can figure out how to build common ground with them so that they like you. It sounds like a gambit to manipulate someone, but it's not. Setting yourself up in a favorable light to increase the chances of most people liking you is a core element to the basic foundation of persuasion.

> ## BE THE CHANGE YOU WANT TO SEE IN THE WORLD
>
> Here's a fact: if you're sending out form messages, *nobody likes you.* Social spamming is the opposite of likeable. Don't do it. Do you like people sending you automated, non-personalized, irrelevant sales messages? Ask yourself, *Would I send this to a friend of a friend?* If the answer is no, you know what to do.

People's emotions toward other people are of paramount importance. Selling isn't just features, benefits, solutions, money, and revenue. It's about people, first and foremost.

Ask yourself, *How can I better humanize the exchange between me and this person?*

DEVELOPING DIGITAL AUTHORITY: SHOW WHAT YOU KNOW

Being an authority on something brings with it innumerable benefits. You secure speaking gigs, you're invited to contribute to articles and podcasts, and you have verified social proof, plus authority that your buyers can trust you.

If you're a sales professional, you have some level of expertise. Whatever you know, you can share it. Even if you don't have a PhD in Rocket Science, to the right buyer that has a need for what you do, your expertise is a window into how you operate and into your mind. It's an organic way to accredit yourself in the eyes of any potential new prospect.

Of course, it's important never to pretend to be an authority or claim that you have a title you don't have, or anything disingenuous. Amplify yourself as an honest and learned authority in a subject with engagement, thought leadership, and consistency. It's a powerful contributor to leveraging your digitally persuasive potential.

MEASURE YOUR SUCCESS

Think about how much the world has changed recently. Ten years ago, you'd check your email once a day from your desktop for maybe an hour. The expected response time on an email was one or two days. Now we have phones in our pockets and purses that are constantly buzzing for our attention. Our digital messaging is a 24/7 open channel.

This is just the beginning. Think about what's going to happen in the next ten years. Can you even imagine where technology is going to take our communication?

You may not be learning skills for the modern marketplace in your sales training class. Your peers might not be, either. It might feel a little bit out of your comfort zone, or a little bit different. But the reality is that the two percent of people who are brave enough, creative enough, and work hard enough are the ones who will rise to the top. You can be one of those people.

PRICE SCHMICE

One of the measures of success is something called *relationship selling*. It's the idea that if you establish a relationship with someone, price doesn't even matter.

For example, one of our clients is a FinTech startup. The CMO and I have built a great relationship, to the point that, recently, she told me, "Hey, we were thinking about how we need to do a better job with increasing our social ad conversions." So, I consulted with my social advertising expert and we brainstormed on how to modify the designs, spend, platforms, etc. I came back to the CMO with three concepts, and she said, "I love this first concept. Let's do it."

She didn't ask how much it cost.

I asked, "Well, do you know how much it costs?"

"Oh, yeah. How much does it cost?"

I steeled myself, then told her, "Well, it's twenty grand."

Not even a pause. "Done. Send me the invoice."

I could have said a hundred grand, or I could have said two grand—it didn't matter. She trusts me, I trust her, and we both knew that I would take care of her because we have a strong relationship that we'd built together. Price didn't matter.

At the end of the day, *you* are the strongest factor in your powers of digital persuasion. Everything I've talked about in this book has one crucial thing in common: *you*. Your messaging, your timing, your intention of service, and your relationship-building are all held together by the glue that is your personality as a Friend and Server. Your success in the modern marketplace is entirely up to you, and it's my hope that you will be brave and creative so you can build the dream.

CONCLUSION

IGNITING INBOUND OPPORTUNITY

There are two main channels of digital persuasion: outbound and inbound.

The outbound format is primarily what this book has been about. The type of content (messages, calls, emails, etc.) that you actively message out to potential buyers.

Inbound persuasion begins to get steam when the buyers approach you first. This happens when you've done such a great job building real relationships that you've gained momentum from your referrals, up-sells, and cross-sells.

The goal of all of these efforts is to create a seismic shift in your sales life so you can move from *outbound* to *inbound* opportunity cultivation. You've built a reputation and a brand. Leveraging the PUB message is how you activate more referrals and word of mouth.

For a long time, I had to do a lot of outreach to get clients to hire us to run social media for their events. I put the digitally persuasive techniques that I'd been using into my posts on social media; I was Personal, Useful, and Brief in all my posts on social and with all our content marketing. It worked—people noticed my messages and appreciated the value I was bringing.

Now I rarely put effort into outbound business development for Socialite. At this point, I've built a scalable business where the majority of my clients come to me. I keep the referral machine humming by writing posts and keeping my social media active and relevant. And you can do the same!

It takes time to get noticed, but the time it takes to go from relying mostly on outbound digital persuasion to relying mostly on inbound is directly correlated to what you put into it. If you're creating helpful content and sending out ten PUB messages to target prospects daily, you're going to have a much faster ramp up toward the shift to inbound. If you only send out a couple messages a day, you may have a slower ramp; but, as long as those messages are quality, you'll still get there.

It's like exercise. You can lose ten pounds over the course of a year, or, if you go nuts, you can lose ten pounds in two months. It just depends on the effort you put in.

The important thing is to be consistent and disciplined. You won't see change all at once. But if you keep with it, suddenly, one day, you'll realize all your clients are coming to you, rather than the other way around.

REJECTION NOT REQUIRED

Tell me if this sounds familiar:

The tougher you are, the better!

Don't let it get to you!

Rejection is just part of the job.

If you're anything like me, you heard those phrases of "encouragement" over and over when you were starting out in sales. You were probably told to be tougher, stronger, and that sales reps who could "get back up off the mat" were the ones who'd succeed.

Oftentimes, there is still an old guard in the world of sales that rewards people for being tough, soulless, and without any feelings. Foes and Sellers win awards in the eyes of management, right?

Becoming more digitally persuasive means thinking about your business in the opposite way. It means positioning yourself as a Friend and a Server. You are a person with a conscience and with feelings, just like your prospects. Your relationships are your revenue. Your network is your net worth. It's emotionally debilitating to be silently rejected online for ninety percent of your day, or whatever amount of time you spent sending messages that don't ignite opportunities. This isn't a healthy way to live, it's not good for you, and if it sounds like the way you're working and living, it doesn't have to be that way!

The formula you've learned in this book eliminates the pain of rejection that comes from old sales scripts and traditional strategies. You don't need to feel rejected every day. *Rejection doesn't have to be a part of the modern salesperson's day.*

With PUB messaging and a mindset of personalization, relationship-building, and anti-automation, rejections go away and opportunities take their place. You get to win, without all the pain. Instead of silence or no, you'll hear maybe and yes.

Yes, more of your messages will get responses than be ignored!

Yes, you'll have better and more long-lasting relationships!

Yes, you'll attract inbound business and build a churning machine of sales opportunity!

When I ask the sales teams I work with what they like best about this digital persuasion formula and modern mindset—that *didn't* have to do with money—this is what they shared:

I get more time with my kids.

I feel proud of my work.

I feel more respected.

I love the relationships I've built.

I don't feel bad about what I do anymore.

I feel like my buyers are my friends.

I feel like my time is well spent, like I'm not wasting it anymore.

My relationships are broader, deeper, and more profitable than ever before.

Imagine a world of business communication where each of us receives what we need and want, and processing our messaging each day made us feel happy, respected, cared-for, and like we'd just quickly caught up with a Friend. That's the kind of world you can live in. You can choose to make it your world.

You are now on the forefront of a powerfully disruptive movement to the classic sales machine that's literally changing the face of business. You can contribute to this positive change while others wonder why they've been left behind.

WHAT'S YOUR NEW STORY?

You have a story to tell. You have a journey you are beginning, enduring, experiencing, or completing. Every time you touch your keyboard, of course, your ultimate goal is to sell more—but just think of your complimentary goals, the people you can meet, the relationships you can build. If you're hammering inboxes with hundreds of uninspired messages, think of all the people you're annoying and you'll never get to know.

Who knows what the missed-opportunity cost of that

approach is? Who knows how many of those people you've annoyed or pissed off or brushed off, without taking the time to make a personalized connection, could have been a valuable relationship? Who knows where that missed opportunity could have led your life financially or emotionally?

Every time I meet someone new from a conversation that started digitally, my *favorite* part is getting to meet them face to face and in person, via video conferencing or at an event. The ability to harness online tools to activate and deepen *offline* actions and relationships is something uniquely available to our moment in time. When I reach out to someone on LinkedIn with a Personal, Useful, Brief message, most of the time, they write back. And if I have a Skype call with them or even meet with them in person, every single person either has an insight or an idea that triggers an amazing new direction in my work and my life. You've probably experienced this yourself.

At any moment, your life is one meeting away from being completely changed. Think about the most impactful meetings that you've had, whether they led to an exciting new job opportunity, a rewarding relationship, or even just a fantastic memory that enriched your professional experience.

Digital persuasion is about humanizing prospects into

people and about improving the kind of salesperson, entrepreneur, or marketer you want to be. You can completely change your life with a few well-placed words and the intention of being a Friend or a Server to someone new.

Tomorrow, after you've made your big cup of coffee and you're ready to sit down and start your workday, take a moment to examine your perspective. Imagine your buyer at that exact moment. What are they doing? What are they thinking? Imagine the message you'd want to read if you were in their shoes. What do you want to see when you open your inbox today?

Every outreach is an opportunity for your voice to be heard. Every message is a moment that could change your life. Every digital composition is a chance to move you closer to achieving your goals.

When you write your next text, social media post, or email, notice that blinking cursor that you may have stopped seeing long ago. With every blink of that cursor, imagine a little light bulb flashing reminding you to "think, think, think." *Is this Personal? Is this Useful? Is this Brief?*

My hope for you is that, moving forward, every single time you touch your phone or keyboard, you will use your new powers of persuasion to positively influence others who have the power to say *yes*.

ABOUT THE AUTHOR

 **ERIN GARGAN** is an award-winning entrepreneur, author, and digital persuasion expert. She is the CEO of Socialite Agency, a social media firm whose clients include the Oscars, ABC/Disney, VISA, Hitachi, Siemens, and others. Erin helps sales, marketing, and event professionals attract attention and increase influence using the power of digital persuasion. To learn more about working with Erin or her team visit www.eringargan.com, www.socialite.agency, or tweet her @eringargan.

83709286R00143